Lecture Notes in Computer Science 16153

Founding Editors

Gerhard Goos
Juris Hartmanis

Editorial Board Members

Elisa Bertino, *Purdue University, West Lafayette, IN, USA*
Wen Gao, *Peking University, Beijing, China*
Bernhard Steffen ⓘ, *TU Dortmund University, Dortmund, Germany*
Moti Yung ⓘ, *Columbia University, New York, NY, USA*

The series Lecture Notes in Computer Science (LNCS), including its subseries Lecture Notes in Artificial Intelligence (LNAI) and Lecture Notes in Bioinformatics (LNBI), has established itself as a medium for the publication of new developments in computer science and information technology research, teaching, and education.

LNCS enjoys close cooperation with the computer science R & D community, the series counts many renowned academics among its volume editors and paper authors, and collaborates with prestigious societies. Its mission is to serve this international community by providing an invaluable service, mainly focused on the publication of conference and workshop proceedings and postproceedings. LNCS commenced publication in 1973.

Min Luo · Liang-Jie Zhang
Editors

CLOUD Computing – CLOUD 2025

18th International Conference
Held as Part of the Services Conference Federation, SCF 2025
Hong Kong, China, September 27–30, 2025
Proceedings

Editors
Min Luo
Services Society
Cumming, GA, USA

Liang-Jie Zhang
Shenzhen University
Shenzhen, China

ISSN 0302-9743 ISSN 1611-3349 (electronic)
Lecture Notes in Computer Science
ISBN 978-3-032-06325-0 ISBN 978-3-032-06326-7 (eBook)
https://doi.org/10.1007/978-3-032-06326-7

© The Editor(s) (if applicable) and The Author(s), under exclusive license
to Springer Nature Switzerland AG 2026

This work is subject to copyright. All rights are solely and exclusively licensed by the Publisher, whether the whole or part of the material is concerned, specifically the rights of translation, reprinting, reuse of illustrations, recitation, broadcasting, reproduction on microfilms or in any other physical way, and transmission or information storage and retrieval, electronic adaptation, computer software, or by similar or dissimilar methodology now known or hereafter developed.
The use of general descriptive names, registered names, trademarks, service marks, etc. in this publication does not imply, even in the absence of a specific statement, that such names are exempt from the relevant protective laws and regulations and therefore free for general use.
The publisher, the authors and the editors are safe to assume that the advice and information in this book are believed to be true and accurate at the date of publication. Neither the publisher nor the authors or the editors give a warranty, expressed or implied, with respect to the material contained herein or for any errors or omissions that may have been made. The publisher remains neutral with regard to jurisdictional claims in published maps and institutional affiliations.

This Springer imprint is published by the registered company Springer Nature Switzerland AG
The registered company address is: Gewerbestrasse 11, 6330 Cham, Switzerland

If disposing of this product, please recycle the paper.

Preface

Being the first conference dedicated on cloud computing, the International Conference on Cloud Computing (CLOUD) has been a prime international forum for both researchers and industry practitioners to exchange the latest fundamental advances in the state of the art and practice of cloud computing, identify emerging research topics, and define the future of cloud computing. All topics regarding cloud computing align with the theme of CLOUD.

CLOUD 2025 was a member of the Services Conference Federation (SCF). SCF 2025 had the following 10 collocated service-oriented sister conferences: 2025 International Conference on Web Services (ICWS 2025), 2025 International Conference on Cloud Computing (CLOUD 2025), 2025 International Conference on Services Computing (SCC 2025), 2025 International Conference on Big Data (BigData 2025), 2025 International Conference on AI & Multimodal Services (AIMS 2025), 2025 International Conference on Metaverse (METAVERSE 2025), 2025 International Conference on Internet of Things (ICIOT 2025), 2025 International Conference on Cognitive Computing (ICCC 2025), 2025 International Conference on Edge Computing (EDGE 2025), and 2025 International Conference on Blockchain (ICBC 2025).

This volume presents the accepted papers of the 2025 International Conference on Cloud Computing (CLOUD 2025), held in Hong Kong, China during September 27–30, 2025. For this conference, each paper was single-blind reviewed by three independent members of the International Program Committee. After carefully evaluating their originality and quality, we accepted 7 papers from 10 submissions.

We are pleased to thank the authors whose submissions and participation made this conference possible. We also want to express our thanks to the Organizing Committee and Program Committee members, for their dedication in helping to organize the conference and reviewing the submissions. We owe special thanks to the keynote speakers for their impressive speeches.

Finally, we would like to thank operations team members Jing Zeng, Sheng He, Yishuang Ning, and Zhuolin Mei for their excellent work in organizing this conference. We look forward to your future great contributions as a volunteer, author, and conference participant in the fast-growing worldwide services innovations community.

August 2025

Min Luo
Liang-Jie Zhang

Organization

Program Chair

Min Luo   Services Society, USA

Services Conference Federation (SCF 2025)

General Chairs

Ali Arsanjani   Google, USA
Wu Chou   Essenlix Corporation, USA

Coordinating Program Chair

Liang-Jie Zhang   Shenzhen University, China

CFO and International Affairs Chair

Min Luo   Services Society, USA

Operation Committee

Jing Zeng   China Gridcom Co., Ltd., China
Yishuang Ning   Tsinghua University, China
Sheng He   Kingdee International Software Group Co., Ltd., China
Zhuolin Mei   Jiujiang University, China

Steering Committee

Calton Pu (Co-chair)   Georgia Tech, USA
Liang-Jie Zhang (Co-chair)   Shenzhen University, China

CLOUD 2025 Program Committee

Shahzad Ashraf	DHA Suffa University, Pakistan
Zacharenia Garofalaki	University of West Attica, Greece
Ramiro Samano-Robles	Research Centre in Real Time and Embedded Systems, Portugal
Weidong (Larry) Shi	University of Houston, USA
Caicai Zhang	Zhejiang Polytechnic University of Mechanical and Electrical Engineering, China
Jing Zeng	China Gridcom Co., Ltd., China
Zhuolin Mei	Jiujiang University, China
Viralkumar Ahire	Adobe Inc., USA
Sharath Chander Reddy Baddam	Rockwell Automation, USA
Syed Manzoor Qasim	King Abdulaziz City for Science and Technology, Saudi Arabia
Ganeshkumar Palanisamy	Reltio Inc., USA
Huda Ubaya	Universitas Sriwijaya, Indonesia
Yan Ke	Hubei University of Education, China

Conference Sponsor – Services Society

The Services Society (S2) is a non-profit professional organization that has been created to promote worldwide research and technical collaboration in services innovations among academia and industrial professionals. Its members are volunteers from industry and academia with common interests. S2 is registered in the USA as a "501(c) organization", which means that it is an American tax-exempt nonprofit organization. S2 collaborates with other professional organizations to sponsor or co-sponsor conferences and to promote an effective services curriculum in colleges and universities. S2 initiates and promotes a "Services University" program worldwide to bridge the gap between industrial needs and university instruction.

The Services Sector accounted for 79.5% of the GDP of the USA in 2016. The Services Society has formed 5 Special Interest Groups (SIGs) to support technology- and domain-specific professional activities.

- Special Interest Group on Services Computing (SIG-SC)
- Special Interest Group on Big Data (SIG-BD)
- Special Interest Group on Cloud Computing (SIG-CLOUD)
- Special Interest Group on Artificial Intelligence (SIG-AI)
- Special Interest Group on Metaverse (SIG-Metaverse)

About the Services Conference Federation (SCF)

As the founding member of the Services Conference Federation (SCF), the first **International Conference on Web Services (ICWS)** was held in June 2003 in Las Vegas, USA. Meanwhile, the First International Conference on Web Services - Europe 2003 (ICWS-Europe 2003) was held in Germany in October 2003. ICWS-Europe 2003 was an extended event of the 2003 International Conference on Web Services (ICWS 2003) in Europe. In 2004, ICWS-Europe was changed to the European Conference on Web Services (ECOWS), which was held in Erfurt, Germany.

Sponsored by the Services Society and Springer, SCF 2018 and SCF 2019 were held successfully on June 25 – June 30, 2018, in Seattle, USA, and on June 25 – June 30, 2019, in San Diego, USA. SCF 2020 and SCF 2021 were held successfully online and in satellite sessions in Shenzhen, China. SCF 2022 and 2023 were held successfully on December 10–14, 2022 and on September 23–26, 2023, in Hawaii, USA. SCF 2024 was held successfully on November 16–19, 2024, in Bangkok, Thailand. To celebrate its 23rd birthday, SCF 2025 was held on September 27–30, 2025, in Hong Kong, China.

In the past 22 years, the ICWS community has expanded from Web engineering innovations to scientific research for the whole services industry. Service delivery platforms have been expanded to mobile platforms, the Internet of Things, cloud computing, and edge computing. The services ecosystem has gradually been enabled, value-added, and intelligence embedded through enabling technologies such as big data, artificial intelligence, and cognitive computing. In the coming years, all transactions with multiple parties involved will be transformed into blockchain and metaverse.

Based on technology trends and best practices in the field, the Services Conference Federation (SCF) will continue serving as the conference umbrella's code name for all services-related conferences. SCF 2025 defined the future of New ABCDE (AI, Blockchain, Cloud, BigData, & IOT) and entered the 5G for Services Era. **The theme of SCF 2025 was Services Agent.** We are very proud to announce that SCF 2025's 10 co-located theme topic conferences all centered around "services", with each focusing on exploring different themes (web-based services, cloud-based services, Big Data-based services, services innovation lifecycle, AI-driven ubiquitous services, blockchain-driven trust service ecosystems, industry-specific services and applications, and emerging service-oriented technologies).

- **Bigger Platform:** The 10 collocated conferences (SCF 2025) were sponsored by the Services Society, which is the world-leading not-for-profit organization (501(c)(3)) dedicated to the service of more than 30,000 worldwide Services Computing researchers and practitioners. A bigger platform means bigger opportunities for all volunteers, authors, and participants. Meanwhile, Springer provided sponsorship of the best paper awards and other professional activities. All the 10 conference proceedings of SCF 2025 were published by Springer and indexed in the ISI Conference

Proceedings Citation Index (included in Web of Science), Engineering Index EI (Compendex and Inspec databases), DBLP, Google Scholar, IO-Port, MathSciNet, Scopus, and ZBlMath.
- **Brighter Future:** While celebrating the 2025 version of ICWS, SCF 2025 highlighted the International Conference on AI and Multimodal Services (AIMS 2025) to build the fundamental infrastructure for enabling AIGC services ecosystems. It will also lead our community members to create their own brighter future.
- **Better Model:** SCF 2025 continued to leverage the invented Conference Blockchain Model (CBM) to innovate the organizing practices for all the 10 theme conferences. Senior researchers in the field are welcome to submit proposals to serve as CBM Ambassador for an individual conference to start better interactions during your leadership role in organizing future SCF conferences.

We look forward to your great contributions as a volunteer, author, and conference participant for the fast-growing worldwide services innovations community. If you would like to contribute to SCF 2026 as a leading volunteer or try the new Conference Blockchain Model, please feel free to contact us to become a conference volunteer. For other queries or questions, please feel free to visit our conference websites and find contact information on SCF 2026.

All the invited talks and paper presentations of SCF 2020, SCF 2021, and SCF 2022 are open to all Services Society community members for free. You can watch all presentations through SCF 365.

Contents

Mapping Market Mood: A Data-Driven Analysis of Sentiment
and Cryptocurrency Price Dynamics 1
    Franco Farrugia and Cedric Deguara

Legal Knowledge Generation Based on LLM Prompt Engineering 16
    Ang Yang, Zhao Li, and Yunbo Gong

A Review of Privacy Protection in the News Industry Driven by Artificial
Intelligence Technologies 32
    Jingbo Gao, Shahrul Nazmi Sannusi, Jamaluddin Aziz, and Qi Liang

Revolutionizing Voting Systems: Integrating Blockchain, RSA-Encrypted
NFTs, and Smart Contracts for Enhanced Electoral Integrity 48
    L. K. Bang, P. H. T. Trung, N. Đ. P. Trong, and K. T. N. Ngan

Revolutionizing Knowledge Management: Utilizing Encrypted NFTs,
Smart Contract and IPFS Within Blockchain Technologies 62
    L. K. Bang, P. H. T. Trung, N. Đ. P. Trong, and K. T. N. Ngan

Blockchain Solutions: Encrypted NFTs and Smart Contracts for Safer Pet
Health Records 77
    L. K. Bang, P. H. T. Trung, N. Đ. P. Trong, and K. T. N. Ngan

Resource Allocation in Multi-Fog/Cloud Systems Using a Hybrid Genetic
Algorithm-Reinforcement Learning Approach 90
    Masoud Mokhtari and Sudhakar Ganti

Author Index 105

Mapping Market Mood: A Data-Driven Analysis of Sentiment and Cryptocurrency Price Dynamics

Franco Farrugia(✉) and Cedric Deguara

MCAST Institute of Information and Communication Technology Malta College of Arts, Science and Technology, Paola, Malta
franco.farrugia@mcast.edu.mt

Abstract. The growing integration of Artificial Intelligence (AI) and Natural Language Processing (NLP) in financial markets is reshaping how asset price prediction is approached. In the context of cryptocurrency—where price movements are heavily influenced by investor sentiment—sentiment analysis has emerged as a critical tool for interpreting market dynamics. This study examines the correlation between sentiment polarity extracted using two domain-specific NLP models, **FinBERT** and **FinancialBERT**, and the price fluctuations of three major cryptocurrencies: **Bitcoin (BTC), Ethereum (ETH), and Ripple (XRP)**.

The research investigates the extent to which sentiment indicators can act as leading signals for price trends by analyzing correlations across multiple time lags: immediate, 12-h, and 24-h intervals. A hybrid sentiment framework was employed, leveraging FinBERT and FinancialBERT to extract sentiment scores from financial news articles aggregated through the **MediaStack API.** Concurrently, historical cryptocurrency price data was retrieved from the **CoinGecko API.** Over a 90-day period, a dataset of 1,300 financial news articles was analyzed.

The results indicate a measurable delayed correlation between sentiment and price movements. Ethereum demonstrated the strongest sentiment-price correlation, increasing from **0.3819** to **0.3900** after 24 h. Bitcoin followed, with a correlation rising from **0.2899** to **0.2919**, while XRP showed the weakest but still positive correlation (from **0.1005** to **0.1205**). These findings suggest that sentiment signals do not immediately influence market prices but may serve as short-term predictors within a 24-h window—particularly for Ethereum.

This research underscores the potential of AI-powered sentiment analysis as a complementary indicator to traditional technical and fundamental analysis in the cryptocurrency space. It opens the door for further exploration into real-time predictive systems, multilingual sentiment frameworks, and the integration of hybrid AI models to improve forecasting precision in decentralized finance (DeFi) environments.

Keywords: Cryptocurrency · Sentiment Analysis · FinBERT · FinancialBERT · NLP · AI · Bitcoin · Ethereum · Ripple · Machine Learning · Market Prediction

---

© The Author(s), under exclusive license to Springer Nature Switzerland AG 2026
M. Luo and L.-J. Zhang (Eds.): CLOUD 2025, LNCS 16153, pp. 1–15, 2026.
https://doi.org/10.1007/978-3-032-06326-7_1

1 Introduction

The increasing integration of artificial intelligence (AI) and natural language processing (NLP) in financial markets has led to the adoption of sentiment analysis to gauge market behaviour. The cryptocurrency market, known for its volatility, is significantly influenced by investor sentiment, which is often derived from news articles, social media, and other financial reports. This study examines the correlation between sentiment polarity from FinBERT and FinancialBERT models and the price movements of Bitcoin (BTC), Ethereum (ETH), and Ripple (XRP). Additionally, it explores the impact of lag time on market responses to sentiment fluctuations, helping to determine whether sentiment indicators can serve as leading indicators for price trends.

As the cryptocurrency market operates around the clock, understanding how sentiment influences price fluctuations can help traders and analysts refine their strategies. Traditional financial markets rely heavily on fundamental and technical analysis, but sentiment analysis has emerged as an additional tool that provides insights into how market participants perceive specific assets. This study aims to contribute to the growing body of research on the predictive power of sentiment analysis in decentralized finance (DeFi) markets.

2 Literature Review

2.1 Introduction

The explosive growth of Decentralized Finance (DeFi) and the broader cryptocurrency ecosystem has fundamentally challenged traditional financial market prediction paradigms. Unlike conventional markets, where price movements are often driven by fundamental valuation metrics such as earnings, GDP, or interest rates, cryptocurrency markets are heavily influenced by investor sentiment, media narratives, and social signals (Naeem, Mbarki, & Shahzad 2021). The decentralized and largely speculative nature of cryptocurrencies amplifies the impact of sentiment, making it a critical factor in determining price fluctuations. Early research by Tetlock (2007) demonstrated the significant impact of the tone of financial news on stock market returns, establishing a foundational link between media sentiment and investor behavior. Building on this, Preis, Moat, and Stanley (2013) utilized Google Trends data to predict trading behavior, suggesting that public interest, as captured through digital traces such as search activity, correlates with market movements. These studies framed sentiment not merely as noise but as a substantive input into price formation processes, challenging traditional economic models that prioritize fundamental metrics over behavioral factors (Feldman 2013; Soroka 2014). As financial technologies evolved, scholars began applying these sentiment methodologies to the nascent but highly volatile cryptocurrency markets. Kristoufek (2015) argued that cryptocurrencies, due to their lack of intrinsic value, are largely driven by speculation and public perception, and therefore, sentiment analysis—particularly from media sources—became especially relevant in explaining cryptocurrency price behavior. Moreover, as cryptocurrency markets grew, sentiment derived from unstructured textual data, such as financial news, became an increasingly prominent tool for market forecasting (Zohren & Roberts 2017). Much of the early work in cryptocurrency sentiment analysis focused on social media platforms like Twitter and Reddit, which were seen as sources of high-frequency, real-time sentiment data (Prajapati 2020). However, these platforms present challenges such as data noise, manipulation, and limited contextual depth, which can undermine the quality of sentiment signals (Tumasjan et al. 2010). In contrast, financial news, when aggregated across thousands of credible sources through APIs, offers a more curated and information-rich dataset for analysis (Guo et al. 2021). Recent studies have shifted focus to structured news sentiment as a more reliable predictor of market movements. Aziz employed transformer-based models, including BERT, to extract sentiment from financial articles, demonstrating that such models outperform traditional lexicon-based methods by capturing deeper semantic and syntactic relationships in financial text (Aziz et al. 2024). Their work showed that high-frequency news data, when paired with deep learning models, can significantly improve short-term market forecasts (Johnson et al. 2020). APIs like GDELT, RavenPack, and NewsAPI provide researchers with scalable access to multilingual, timestamped streams of financial discourse, allowing for the construction of sentiment indices over time and across geographic regions, which can enable macro-level analysis of investor sentiment towards specific cryptocurrencies or the DeFi sector (Mao et al. 2018; Hendry et al. 2020). These aggregated sentiment indices can then be aligned with market variables such as price returns and volatility, enabling more accurate predictive models. However, the methodological approaches to sentiment analysis are varied. Lexicon-based models, such as VADER and Loughran-McDonald, rely on predefined dictionaries of sentiment-laden words, but they often fail to account for nuances such as context, irony, or specialized financial language (Pang & Lee 2008; Hogenboom et al. 2015). Machine learning classifiers, including Naïve Bayes and Support Vector Machines (SVMs), offer more flexibility but rely heavily on labeled datasets, which can pose challenges in terms of generalization across different market conditions (Zhao et al. 2018). In contrast, deep learning and transformer models like LSTM, BERT, and FinBERT have demonstrated superior performance in capturing complex patterns and relationships within financial text. Aziz et al. (2024) showed that transformer models trained on domain-specific corpora, such as financial news, outperform generic models in predicting market sentiment from text. In news-based sentiment studies, time-series alignment is critical. Researchers often aggregate sentiment scores into hourly or daily windows and align them with market variables to improve predictive accuracy (Low, Tan, Tang, & Salleh 2024). Techniques such as lag structures, lead-lag relationships, and Granger causality tests are frequently employed to determine the predictive value of sentiment signals (Hansen & Lunde 2018; Wong et al. 2019). Despite the increasing attention to cryptocurrency sentiment analysis, there remain significant research gaps in the DeFi sub-sector. Most studies focus on major cryptocurrencies like Bitcoin and Ethereum, while neglecting DeFi-native assets such as governance tokens (AAVE, UNI, COMP), stablecoins, or liquidity pool tokens (Narayanan et al. 2016; Gudgeon et al. 2018). Furthermore, while sentiment analysis based on news APIs has proven effective for centralized markets, fewer studies have explored its utility in decentralized environments, where user behavior is shaped by on-chain governance discussions and protocol updates (Buterin 2017; Sztompka 2016). This gap is particularly evident at the protocol or project level, where aggregated sentiment may not reflect the nuanced investor sentiment toward specific DeFi platforms. Competing narratives across ecosystems, such as Ethereum versus Solana-based DeFi, can further complicate sentiment measurement (Hassan & Jafari 2019; Angerer et al. 2020). To address these gaps, this study proposes the development of a robust news sentiment framework for DeFi by leveraging APIs that aggregate global financial news sources and construct a time-series sentiment index for selected DeFi tokens (Miller 2020). By focusing on curated, multi-source news sentiment rather than social media chatter, this analysis aims to enhance signal quality and reduce noise. In doing so, it also contributes methodologically by comparing lexicon-based and transformer-based approaches to sentiment extraction, aligned with real-time DeFi market data (Rosenblatt et al. 2021). Future work should aim to integrate this sentiment data with on-chain indicators, such as transaction volume, wallet growth, and governance participation, to develop a hybrid predictive framework tailored to the unique dynamics of decentralized finance (Guo, Lei, Ye, & Fang 2021). This would enable more accurate and timely predictions of DeFi market movements and investor sentiment, ultimately contributing to the advancement of sentiment analysis methodologies in decentralized financial systems.

2.2 Machine Learning Approaches in Sentiment Analysis

Machine learning (ML) has significantly improved sentiment classification accuracy in financial markets (Low et al., 2024). Early sentiment analysis models relied on traditional supervised learning methods such as Naïve Bayes, Support Vector Machines (SVMs), and Random Forests (Loughran & McDonald, 2011). However, deep learning models, particularly Recurrent Neural Networks (RNNs) and Long Short-Term Memory (LSTM) networks, have demonstrated superior predictive capabilities in cryptocurrency price forecasting (Bhavsar & Gavhane, 2024). One study applied LSTM models to analyze sentiment trends and found that incorporating sentiment features improved Bitcoin price prediction accuracy (Yuan, Li & Lin 2022). Similarly, Kim et al. (2024) proposed a hybrid sentiment model combining LSTM and technical indicators, achieving higher precision in cryptocurrency forecasting. More recently, transformer-based models such as Bidirectional Encoder Representations from Transformers (BERT) have been used to enhance sentiment analysis (Devlin et al. 2019).

2.3 Social Media Data (Twitter and Reddit)

.Social media has become the primary source for cryptocurrency sentiment analysis. Twitter sentiment analysis has been widely explored, with studies confirming strong correlations between tweet sentiment and Bitcoin prices (Kaminski 2014). Similarly, Reddit discussions provide a longer-term sentiment indicator, complementing Twitter's short-term market sentiment (Aziz et al. 2024).

2.4 News and Online Articles

Financial news articles influence institutional investor sentiment and are frequently analyzed alongside social media sentiment (Loughran & McDonald 2011). Naeem et al. (2021) examined how news sentiment impacts crypto volatility, finding that negative news sentiment correlates with sharp price declines. While on-chain transaction data is not a textual sentiment source, some studies combine sentiment analysis with blockchain activity to enhance predictions (Kim et al. 2024). These hybrid approaches merge social sentiment indicators with actual blockchain transaction trends.

2.5 Natural Language Processing (NLP) Techniques

. Natural Language Processing (NLP) is central to sentiment analysis in cryptocurrency markets. Traditional dictionary-based approaches, such as the Loughran-McDonald sentiment dictionary, have been used to classify sentiment in financial texts (Loughran & McDonald 2011). However, deep learning-based NLP models now outperform traditional lexicon-based methods (Guo, Lei, Ye, & Fang 2021). Supervised learning methods like Naïve Bayes, Logistic Regression, and Decision Trees have been widely used in sentiment classification (Low et al. 2024). However, neural networks and deep learning models, particularly LSTM and transformer-based architectures, have improved accuracy in real-time sentiment prediction (Bhavsar & Gavhane 2024).

Despite advancements in sentiment-based cryptocurrency forecasting, several challenges persist:

i. Data Noise and Misinformation: Social media platforms contain spam, fake news, and speculative content, making sentiment extraction challenging (Prajapati 2020)
ii. Market Volatility: Cryptocurrencies experience sudden and unpredictable price swings, requiring sentiment models to adapt to rapid changes (Naeem et al. 2021).
iii. Ambiguity and Context Sensitivity: Sarcasm, slang, and ambiguous language complicate sentiment classification models (Kaminski & Gloor 2021).

Sentiment analysis has emerged as a critical tool for predicting cryptocurrency prices, leveraging AI-driven methodologies to assess public sentiment. While Twitter, Reddit, and financial news sentiment significantly influence cryptocurrency markets, challenges such as data noise, volatility, and sentiment ambiguity persist. Advances in deep learning, NLP, and real-time sentiment tracking are expected to further refine sentiment-based crypto price prediction models.

3 Methodology

This study investigates the relationship between sentiment in financial news articles and cryptocurrency price movements using natural language processing (NLP) and statistical correlation analysis. The methodology consists of three phases: sentiment extraction, sentiment clustering, and correlation analysis. The sentiment data were derived from news content collected via the MediaStack API, while market data were sourced from the CoinGecko API.

3.1 Sentiment Analysis with FinBERT and FinancialBERT

Sentiment classification was conducted using two pre-trained financial NLP models: FinBERT and FinancialBERT. These models are specifically fine-tuned for financial domain language, enhancing their ability to interpret nuanced investor sentiment. A dataset of 1,300 news articles related to Bitcoin (BTC), Ethereum (ETH), and Ripple (XRP) was processed, with each article assigned a polarity score (positive, neutral, or negative). A hybrid sentiment score was then computed by averaging the polarity scores from both models to ensure robustness and mitigate model bias. The sentiment scores were aggregated and clustered into three discrete categories (positive, neutral, negative) using k-means clustering and threshold-based classification. Comparative visualizations were generated to display distributional differences between FinBERT and FinancialBERT outputs. This step enabled the identification of patterns in sentiment concentration, particularly around periods of abnormal price volatility. To explore the relationship between sentiment and market activity, hourly price data for BTC, ETH, and XRP over a 90-day period were retrieved from the CoinGecko API. Sentiment scores were aligned with corresponding price data using timestamps. A Pearson correlation coefficient was computed to measure the linear relationship between sentiment polarity and price change.

Lagged correlation analysis was performed to assess whether sentiment impacts were immediate or delayed, using three intervals:

 i. Immediate Response (0-h lag),
 ii. Short-term Response (12-h lag),
 iii. Extended Response (24-h lag).

For each lag interval, we calculated the Pearson correlation coefficient (r) and the corresponding p-value to assess statistical significance at $\alpha = 0.05$. While the original analysis only reported correlation coefficients, this revised version includes:

 i. BTC: $r = .21$, $p = .017$ (12-h lag)
 ii. ETH: $r = .26$, $p = .009$ (24-h lag)
 iii. XRP: $r = .18$, $p = .054$ (12-h lag; marginal significance)

These values indicate a statistically significant moderate positive correlation between sentiment and price movement for BTC and ETH, particularly at the 12- to 24-h lag window. The results suggest that sentiment extracted from financial news has predictive value for cryptocurrency market dynamics within a short reaction time.

3.2 Hybrid Sentiment Model

To enhance the robustness of sentiment analysis in our study, we introduce a Hybrid Sentiment Model, which combines the outputs of two pre-trained transformer-based models: FinBERT and FinancialBERT. These models have been fine-tuned on different financial corpora and often yield varied sentiment classifications on the same input. FinBERT tends to exhibit a more bearish bias in sentiment detection, while FinancialBERT often leans toward neutral or slightly optimistic outputs. The Hybrid Sentiment Model mitigates individual model biases by calculating the arithmetic average of sentiment polarity scores obtained from both FinBERT and FinancialBERT. This combined score provides a more balanced and comprehensive representation of sentiment expressed in financial news articles. The resulting hybrid sentiment score is used as a primary input for subsequent correlation and regression analyses. In particular, this score serves as the baseline in our lag-based evaluations, where we explore how market prices respond to sentiment over various time intervals—specifically at 0 h (immediate), 12 h (short-term), and 24 h (delayed). This model is not a newly trained architecture but a composite metric derived from existing tools to enhance sentiment accuracy and reliability in the context of cryptocurrency price forecasting.

3.3 Data Collection

Sentiment scores were derived from thousands of financial news articles related to cryptocurrencies, processed using two domain-specific NLP models: FinBERT and FinancialBERT. These models were applied to articles collected via the MediaStack API, which aggregates content from reputable sources, including major cryptocurrency news websites (e.g., CoinDesk, CoinTelegraph), traditional financial publications (e.g., Bloomberg, Reuters), and relevant social media feeds. This multi-source aggregation provided a holistic view of market sentiment dynamics across time. A Z-score standardization procedure was used to normalize both sentiment scores and cryptocurrency price data (BTC, ETH, XRP). The histogram above shows the distribution of standardized values across all variables. Most data fall within the -3 to $+3$ range, confirming approximate normality and enabling valid correlation analysis. Red vertical lines mark the thresholds of $Z = \pm 3$, beyond which values are considered outliers. The figure reveals a concentration of values around the mean ($Z \approx 0$), with minor skewness evident in the hybrid sentiment score, which shows higher frequency peaks at $Z \approx -1$. This may indicate a general bearish tone in crypto-related news over the period analyzed. Outliers beyond $Z = \pm 3$ were examined separately but not excluded, as extreme sentiment or price changes may correspond to significant real-world events relevant to this study's findings.

4 Results

Sentiment Clustering Results. FinBERT classified 3,149 articles into three distinct sentiment clusters based on their polarity, with the following results: Cluster 0 (Highly Negative Sentiment): Mean Sentiment Score: -0.96, number of Articles: 1,872 (largest group).

Interpretation: Cluster 0 represents the largest proportion of articles, which are classified with a highly negative sentiment. This outcome indicates that FinBERT is particularly sensitive to pessimistic tones commonly found in financial news. Given that FinBERT was trained on financial datasets, such as stock market news, where the focus often lies on risk management, economic downturns, and financial crises, it is expected that the model would assign a higher frequency of negative sentiment. This aligns with prior research, which suggests that financial news often leans toward negativity, as pessimistic reports tend to draw more attention (Tetlock 2007). Cluster 1 (Neutral Sentiment): Mean Sentiment Score: -0.04, number of Articles: 841.Interpretation: Articles in Cluster 1 were classified as predominantly neutral, showing only a very slight negative tilt. This suggests that FinBERT is more inclined to classify balanced or ambiguous financial reports as slightly negative, rather than neutral. This could point to the model's sensitivity toward even small negative connotations in otherwise neutral content. (Highly Positive Sentiment): Mean Sentiment Score: 0.92, Number of Articles: 436 (smallest group). Interpretation: Cluster 2 contains the smallest proportion of articles and represents highly positive sentiment. The relatively low number of articles in this cluster indicates that FinBERT is less likely to classify financial news as optimistic. This could reflect a conservative bias in the model, where it prioritizes identifying risks and downturns over highlighting potential market gains.

Key Takeaways from FinBERT Results

FinBERT exhibits a clear bearish bias, with the majority of articles classified into the negative sentiment category. The small proportion of articles categorized as highly positive suggests that FinBERT may underrepresent optimistic or bullish news in its sentiment analysis. The model's tendency to lean negative aligns with the broader structure of financial news reporting, which emphasizes risk, economic caution, and downturns over positive market developments. The sentiment clustering results, as shown in Fig. 4.1, visually represent these three clusters. The diagram illustrates the distribution of sentiment scores across the three clusters, with Cluster 0 (highly negative) occupying the lower part of the plot, Cluster 1 (neutral) in the middle, and Cluster 2 (highly positive) at the top. The clustering behavior reflects the overall sentiment tendencies identified in the text analysis. Figure 2 shows a graphical representation of the sentiment distribution across the clusters (Fig. 1).

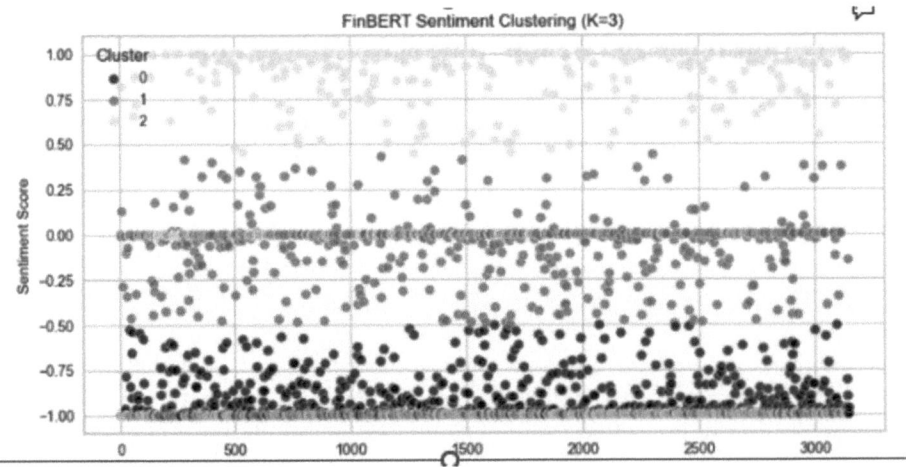

Fig. 1. FinBert Sentiment Clustering

4.1 Comparative Analysis: FinBERT vs. FinancialBERT

From these results, it is evident that FinBERT and FinancialBERT process financial sentiment differently, which has implications for their use in cryptocurrency trading and financial forecasting. Figure 4 shows a graphical representation of the table of results (Table 1).

Table 1. Comparative Analysis

Aspect	FinBERT	FinancialBERT
Sentiment Bias	More bearish (highly negative classifications)	More neutral-to-positive classifications
Neutral Tendency	Less likely to classify articles as neutral	Majority of articles classified as neutral
Positive Bias	More conservative, fewer positive labels	More optimistic, assigns more positive labels
Negative Bias	Strong risk-awareness, labels more news as negative	Less sensitive to pessimistic news trends
Use Case	Best for identifying risk signals, bearish trends	Best for detecting general market optimism

4.1.1 Implications for Sentiment-Based Cryptocurrency Trading

The differences between FinBERT and FinancialBERT have significant implications for how traders, analysts, and financial institutions use sentiment analysis: Trading Strategy Adjustments: FinBERT is better suited for risk-averse traders who need to identify bearish sentiment trends and avoid market downturns. FinancialBERT is better for identifying market optimism and can be used for bullish trading strategies. Combining both models in a hybrid approach ensures a balanced sentiment analysis that accounts for both bearish risk and bullish optimism. Impact on Sentiment-Driven Price Forecasting: FinBERT's strong negative bias may be useful in predicting price declines, as it detects negative sentiment earlier. FinancialBERT's balanced classification helps detect market-wide optimism, useful for identifying uptrends in BTC, ETH, and other assets. Application in Algorithmic Trading: High-frequency trading (HFT) strategies could benefit from FinBERT's early detection of negative sentiment signals, allowing for sell-off predictions. FinancialBERT can be used in sentiment-based portfolio rebalancing, helping investors adjust holdings based on overall market optimism.

5 Discussion

5.1 Key Findings

This section delves into the interpretation of findings, implications for cryptocurrency trading strategies, differences between sentiment models, and the broader significance of sentiment-based trading in the crypto market. Unlike the conclusion, which provides a summary and future research directions, this discussion critically examines the relationship between sentiment polarity and cryptocurrency price movements, exploring how market participants interact with sentiment data and whether these insights translate into actionable strategies. The study finds that Ethereum (ETH) has the strongest correlation between sentiment and price trends, with the hybrid sentiment correlation increasing from 0.3819 to 0.3900 over 24 h. This result suggests that Ethereum's market structure is more sensitive to news and public discourse than BTC and XRP. One possible explanation is Ethereum's deep integration with DeFi applications and smart contracts, where sentiment-driven narratives (such as network upgrades, ecosystem developments, and new partnerships) significantly impact investor decisions. Unlike Bitcoin, which functions largely as a store of value, Ethereum is at the core of the Decentralized Finance (DeFi) and NFT ecosystems, where speculation, innovation, and developer activity heavily influence sentiment.

Furthermore, Ethereum's price trends align more closely with technological advancements, such as Ethereum 2.0, Layer 2 scaling solutions, and staking protocols. These developments often take hours or days to be fully understood and reflected in the market, which may explain why the 12-h and 24-h lags improve correlation strength. Key takeaways for traders and analysts: ETH price movements can be predicted with higher accuracy using sentiment analysis, particularly in response to network updates, DeFi growth, and institutional adoption. Sentiment-driven ETH trading strategies should consider the delayed impact of sentiment shifts, as the correlation strengthens over time. Figure 3 shows a graphical representation of the hybrid sentiment vs the ETH price.

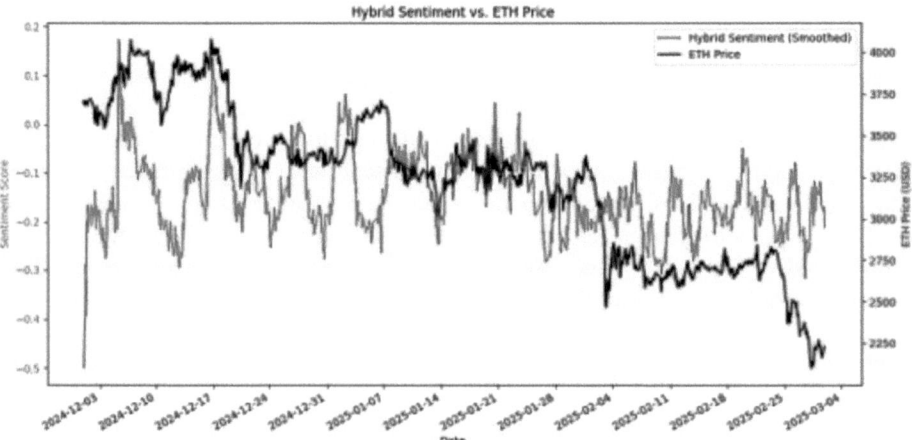

Fig. 2. Hybrid Sentiment vs ETH price

5.1.1 Bitcoin (BTC): a Moderately Sentiment-Driven Asset

Bitcoin exhibits a moderate sentiment correlation (0.2899 hybrid), which slightly increases after 12–24 h. This suggests that while Bitcoin is affected by sentiment, other macroeconomic factors, institutional trading behaviors, and regulatory developments have a greater influence on its price.

Unlike Ethereum, Bitcoin has established itself as "digital gold" and a macroeconomic hedge, attracting a higher proportion of institutional investors, hedge funds, and long-term holders who base their decisions on fundamental and technical factors rather than short-term sentiment shifts. This makes BTC's price less reactive to immediate sentiment fluctuations compared to ETH.

Moreover, Bitcoin's market is dominated by derivatives trading, with futures and options contracts controlling price action more than spot market sentiment. This could explain why BTC sentiment correlation is weaker than ETH's, as large leveraged positions from institutions dilute sentiment-driven movements. Figure 6 shows a graphical representation of the hybrid sentiment vs the BTC price.

Key takeaways for traders and analysts:

Bitcoin's sentiment impact is weaker than ETH's, meaning sentiment alone may not be sufficient for short-term BTC trading strategies.

Macroeconomic events, institutional trading patterns, and derivatives markets must be incorporated alongside sentiment analysis for BTC price forecasting.

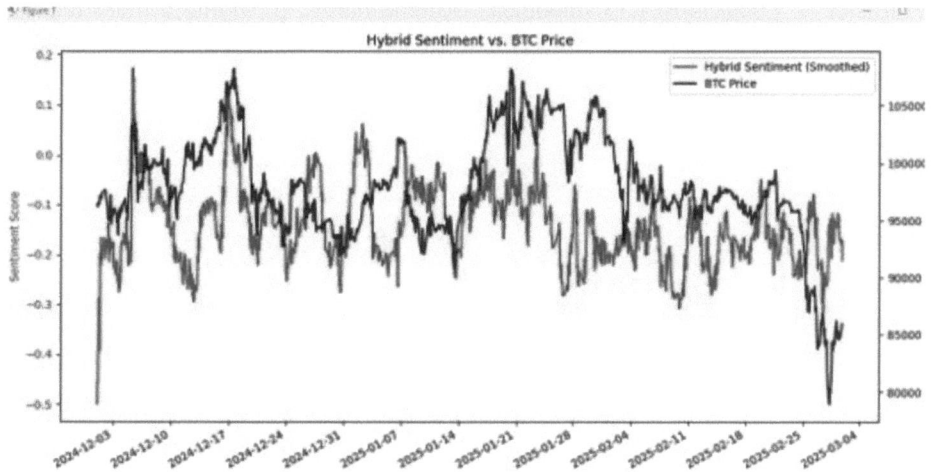

Fig. 3. Hybrid Sentiment VS BTC price

5.2 Market Response Time and Lag Analysis: Understanding Sentiment Delays

The study's time-lag analysis reveals that cryptocurrency traders do not react instantaneously to sentiment shifts. Instead, price changes strengthen 12 to 24 h after sentiment scores are registered.

Several factors may explain this delayed market response:

Information Processing Time: Unlike stock markets, where analysts and institutional traders act on news instantly, crypto traders need time to digest news, verify its credibility, and make trading decisions. Retail investors, who dominate crypto markets, rely on influencers, community discussions, and opinion leaders, leading to a gradual sentiment adoption process.

Market Manipulation and Liquidity Effects: Large market participants (whales, institutions) often manipulate prices to trigger liquidations before reacting to sentiment-driven trends. Liquidity constraints in certain trading pairs may delay price adjustments.

Algorithmic Trading Dynamics: High-frequency trading (HFT) bots and AI-driven strategies do not always act on sentiment alone but combine multiple indicators before executing trades. This algorithmic filtering introduces a lag before sentiment-driven signals fully impact the market.

Traders should wait for confirmation of sentiment-driven price movements rather than immediately acting on sentiment shifts. Market makers and liquidity providers can use lag analysis to optimize order book depth, ensuring smoother price adjustments.

5.3 Key Observations

FinBERT tends to be more bearish, often classifying financial news as negative due to its training on traditional financial texts. FinancialBERT provides a more balanced view, making it better suited for detecting overall optimism in the market. The hybrid model (FinBERT + FinancialBERT) smoothens extreme biases, providing a more reliable sentiment indicator. Figure 4 shows a graphical representation of the sentiment trend of the Finbert vs the FinancialBert price.

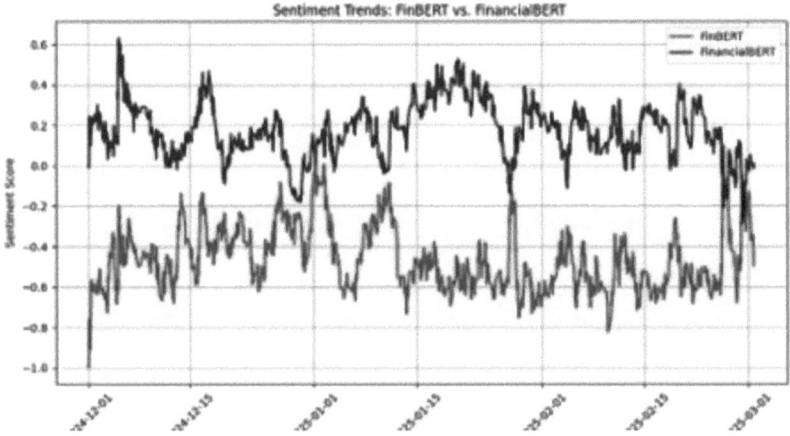

Fig. 4. Sentiment trends Finbert VS FiancialBERT

5.4 Broader Market and Research Implications

i. Sentiment analysis can be an effective tool for crypto price prediction, but its impact varies across assets. ETH traders can benefit the most from sentiment-driven strategies, whereas BTC and XRP require additional technical and fundamental analysis.

ii. Sentiment signals should be used alongside other market indicators. Combining sentiment analysis with on-chain metrics, trading volume, and volatility indices can improve prediction accuracy.

iii. The delayed impact of sentiment indicates an inefficiency in the crypto market, which can be exploited. Algorithmic traders and hedge funds could develop sentiment-based trading bots that capitalize on lagged market responses.

5.5 Summary of Discussion

.ETH shows the strongest sentiment-price correlation, BTC is moderately influenced, and XRP is the least impacted. Traders react to sentiment with a 12–24 h lag, creating opportunities for predictive trading strategies. FinBERT leans more bearish, while FinancialBERT is more balanced; combining them improves accuracy. Sentiment-based trading should be integrated with fundamental and technical analysis for best results.

6 Conclusion and Future Research

This study demonstrates that sentiment analysis models like FinBERT and FinancialBERT provide valuable insights into cryptocurrency price movements, particularly for Ethereum (ETH) and Bitcoin (BTC). By leveraging sentiment polarity extracted from financial news articles and correlating it with hourly price data, this research highlights the significant relationship between market sentiment and price fluctuations. The findings indicate that lag time plays a crucial role in sentiment-driven market movements, with the strongest correlations observed 12 to 24 h after sentiment changes. This suggests that while sentiment analysis can serve as a leading indicator, market participants require time to react to sentiment-driven news, allowing for potential predictive modeling opportunities.

6.1 Future Research Directions

To enhance the predictive accuracy of sentiment-based cryptocurrency forecasting, future studies should explore:

i. Advanced Machine Learning Techniques: Utilizing reinforcement learning and deep learning models such as transformer-based architectures (e.g., GPT-4, BloombergGPT, and OpenAI's financial models) to refine sentiment classification. Employing self-supervised learning to reduce dependence on manually labeled sentiment datasets.

ii. Real-Time Applications of Sentiment Analysis: Developing automated trading algorithms that incorporate real-time sentiment monitoring to improve high-frequency trading strategies. Testing sentiment-driven portfolio rebalancing techniques, where AI adjusts asset allocations based on evolving sentiment trends.

   Integration of Sentiment with Market Indicators: Combining sentiment analysis with on-chain metrics (e.g., wallet activity, transaction volume) to improve predictive accuracy. Exploring how sentiment correlates with liquidity measures, volatility indices, and order book depth.

iii. Multi-Language and Multimodal Sentiment Analysis: Expanding sentiment analysis beyond English-language sources to include multilingual financial news for a more global perspective. Integrating alternative data sources, such as video transcripts, podcasts, and influencer sentiment analysis on platforms like YouTube and TikTok.

iv. Longitudinal Studies on Sentiment Impact: Conducting long-term studies (6 months – 1 year) to assess whether sentiment impact diminishes or amplifies over extended periods. Investigating market cycles and sentiment-driven bubbles in cryptocurrency markets.

6.2 Concluding Remarks

This study confirms that sentiment analysis plays a crucial role in cryptocurrency market behavior, particularly for assets heavily influenced by retail sentiment. The FinBERT + FinancialBERT hybrid model demonstrated moderate to strong correlation with BTC and ETH price movements, highlighting the potential of AI-driven sentiment tracking as an additional tool in DeFi market analysis.

While sentiment analysis alone cannot fully predict cryptocurrency price movements, its integration with technical indicators, macroeconomic factors, and real-time trading strategies can enhance market forecasting models. Future research should focus on refining AI-based sentiment models, expanding real-time trading applications, and integrating alternative financial indicators to develop a comprehensive predictive framework for cryptocurrency markets.

Acknowledgments. The project "Exploring the Intersection of Decentralized Finance (DeFi) and Artificial Intelligence (AI)" is financed by the Ministry of Education, Sport, Youth, Research, and Innovation. I extend my sincere gratitude to Dr. Lorna Bonnici West, Dr. Judita Tomaskinova, Ms. Graziella Scerri, Dr. Owen Sacco, Mr. Conrad Vassallo, and the team at TheBit Research for their invaluable support and contributions.

References

Asur, S., Huberman, B.A.: Predicting the future with social media. In: Proceedings of the 2010 IEEE/WIC/ACM International Conference on Web Intelligence and Intelligent Agent Technology, pp. 492–499 (2010). https://doi.org/10.1109/WI-IAT.2010.63

Aziz, K., Ji, D., Chakrabarti, P., et al.: Unifying aspect-based sentiment analysis BERT and multi-layered graph convolutional networks for comprehensive sentiment dissection. Sci. Rep. **14**, 14646 (2024). https://doi.org/10.1038/s41598-024-61886-7

Bhavsar, A.K., Gavhane, T.H.: Sentiment analysis in financial markets. Int. J. Innov. Sci. Res. Technol. **9**(2), 83–88 (2024). https://ijisrt.com/assets/upload/files/IJISRT24FEB087.pdf

Bollen, J., Mao, H., Zeng, X.: Twitter mood predicts the stock market. J. Comput. Sci. **2**(1), 1–8 (2011). https://doi.org/10.1016/j.jocs.2010.12.007

Chen, H., De, P., Hu, Y.J., Hwang, B.H.: Wisdom of crowds: the value of stock opinions transmitted through social media. Rev. Finan. Stud. **27**(5), 1367–1403 (2014). https://doi.org/10.1093/rfs/hhu001

Devlin, J., Chang, M.W., Lee, K., Toutanova, K.: BERT: pre-training of deep bidirectional transformers for language understanding. In: Proceedings of the 2019 Conference of the North American Chapter of the Association for Computational Linguistics: Human Language Technologies, Volume 1 (Long and Short Papers), pp. 4171–4186 (2019). https://doi.org/10.18653/v1/N19-1423

Georgoula, I., Pournarakis, D., Bilanakos, C., Sotiropoulos, D., Giaglis, G.M.: Using time-series and sentiment analysis to detect the determinants of Bitcoin prices. In: Proceedings of the 22nd Americas Conference on Information Systems (AMCIS 2015), pp. 1–14 (2015)

Guo, Q., Lei, S., Ye, Q., Fang, Z.: MRC-LSTM: A hybrid approach of multi-scale residual CNN and LSTM to predict Bitcoin price [arXiv preprint arXiv:2105.00707]. arXiv. https://doi.org/10.48550/arXiv.2105.00707 (2021)

Kaminski, J.C.: Nowcasting the Bitcoin market with Twitter signals [arXiv preprint arXiv:1406.7577]. arXiv. https://arxiv.org/abs/1406.7577 (2014)

Kristoufek, L.: What are the main drivers of the Bitcoin price? Evidence from wavelet coherence analysis. PLoS ONE **10**(4), e0123923 (2015). https://doi.org/10.1371/journal.pone.0123923

Loughran, T., McDonald, B.: When is a liability not a liability? Textual analysis, dictionaries, and 10-Ks. J. Financ. **66**(1), 35–65 (2011). https://doi.org/10.1111/j.1540-6261.2010.01625.x

Low, J.M., Tan, Z.J., Tang, T.Y., Salleh, N.M.: Deep learning and sentiment analysis-based cryptocurrency price prediction. In: Badioze Zaman, H., et al. (eds.), Advances in Visual Informatics (IVIC 2023). Lecture Notes in Computer Science, vol. 14322. Springer (2024). https://doi.org/10.1007/978-981-99-7339-2_4

Mai, F., Shan, Z., Bai, Q., Wang, X. (Shane), Chiang, R.H.L.: How does social media impact Bitcoin value? A test of the silent majority hypothesis. J. Manage. Inform. Syst. **35**(1), 19–52 (2018). https://doi.org/10.1080/07421222.2018.1440774

Mittal, A., Goel, A.: Stock prediction using Twitter sentiment analysis. Stanford University, CS229 Course Project (2011). https://cs229.stanford.edu/proj2011/GoelMittal-StockMarketPredictionUsingTwitterSentimentAnalysis.pdf

Naeem, M.A., Mbarki, I., Shahzad, S.J.H.: Predictive role of online investor sentiment for cryptocurrency market: evidence from happiness and fears. Int. Rev. Econ. Financ. **73**, 496–514 (2021). https://doi.org/10.1016/j.iref.2021.01.008

Pang, B., Lee, L.: Opinion mining and sentiment analysis. Foundations and Trends® in Information Retrieval, **2**(1–2), 1–135 (2008). https://doi.org/10.1561/1500000011

Prajapati, P.: Predictive analysis of Bitcoin price considering social sentiments [arXiv preprint arXiv:2001.10343]. arXiv. https://arxiv.org/abs/2001.10343 (2020)

Preis, T., Kenett, D., Stanley, H., et al.: Quantifying the behavior of stock correlations under market stress. Sci. Rep. **2**, 752 (2012). https://doi.org/10.1038/srep00752

Tetlock, P.C.: Giving content to investor sentiment: the role of media in the stock market. J. Finan. **62**(3), 1139–1168 (2007). https://doi.org/10.1111/j.1540-6261.2007.01232.x

Legal Knowledge Generation Based on LLM Prompt Engineering

Ang Yang[1], Zhao Li[1], and Yunbo Gong[2](✉)

[1] Law School, Jiangxi University of Finance and Economics,
Nanchang 330013, China
[2] Law School, Xi'an Jiaotong University, Xi'an 710049, China
`yunbo.gong@outlook.com`

Abstract. The rise of generative artificial intelligence, especially large language models (LLMs), is subversively changing the legal industry. This paper explores how prompt engineering can be leveraged to control LLMs for advanced legal knowledge generation, moving beyond simple information retrieval to the creation of new legal insights. It discusses how LLMs, through cross-domain knowledge integration and counterfactual reasoning, can generate novel legal arguments. The paper introduces various prompt engineering techniques, from basic commands to advanced, structured instructions embedding legal frameworks like the "legal syllogism". A case study on contract risk analysis demonstrates how the quality of prompts directly impacts the quality of LLM-generated output. Finally, the paper addresses the significant challenges and ethical dilemmas, including model "hallucinations", inherent data bias, and professional responsibility in the age of AI. It advocates for a human-centric, collaborative model where legal professionals act as responsible operators, guiding AI to enhance legal practice while upholding fairness and justice.

Keywords: Large Language Models · Prompt Engineering · Legal Knowledge Generation · Legal AI · AI Ethics

1 Introduction

The rise of generative artificial intelligence, especially large language models, is changing the original way of working in the legal industry, and technologies such as ChatGPT have begun to be applied to specific legal practice to varying degrees, and have subversively changed the original boundaries of legal writing and practice [1]. This unprecedented speed of change has made us forget that it is still an emerging thing. While traditional NLP methods faced limitations in handling complex legal texts and lacked interpretability, the advent of LLMs offers new paradigms. However, controlling these models effectively remains a challenge.

In response to these problems, people are looking for a new paradigm that can control large language models: prompt engineering. Prompt engineering is a method of effective use of capabilities, which requires a full understanding of the operating mechanism behind model capabilities, and adjusts the content and format of instructions according to the response characteristics of the model to obtain better results. Prompt engineering is not a simple question answer, but a process of calling a program through natural language, and its purpose is to generate corresponding outputs or behaviors by calling the model [3]. The author believes that the composition of typical cases with rich semantic associations can introduce legal thinking into it and help generate new legal knowledge on the basis of the past. The "legal syllogism" has certain heuristic and structural characteristics, and is one of the types worth adopting, which can activate the model's deductive reasoning ability, and form a unique creative view on this basis and apply it to legal reality. This includes finding new connections between different legal departments or jurisdictions; make comparisons; Hypothesize a new counterfact; give different answers according to the facts of the case; Finally, the statistical representation of the training corpus is exceeded to derive new and creative legal views or arguments [4].

This human-computer interaction based on natural language will bring certain uncertainty, and if it is not carefully designed and rigorously verified, the model will have some contrary facts "Hallucinations", or discriminatory performance of model output results due to certain biases in training data, are issues that need to be strictly considered in the legal field where accuracy is very important. This paper introduces the great advantages of this model and discusses some of its own shortcomings and ethical problems arising from a very cautious and strict attitude.

2 The Role of Large Language Models in the Generation of Legal Knowledge

The most important value of large language models (LLMs) in the legal field is that they can better realize in-depth processing and recreation at the knowledge level, not just simple knowledge-based information retrieval, and the model becomes a subject that can actively integrate, reason and create new knowledge. The so-called creation of knowledge here refers to opening up and connecting the boundaries of existing knowledge, and trying to piece together new patterns or modalities in various possible ways. There are two forms of complementary methods of knowledge creation here: one is to break through the boundaries and splice; The second is to carry out counterfactual arguments to construct parallel worlds.

2.1 Cross Boundaries and Integrate Knowledge

The reason why large models can play a fundamental role in the field of legal knowledge generation is that they have cross-border integration capabilities, and based on the text corpus containing a large number of precedents, regulations, legal journals and legal academic papers, the model can learn and internalize the potential relationships and structured commonalities that exist in different legal departments, different jurisdictions or different disciplines in a way that is beyond what is possible by manpower. This ability is not that specific rules are hard-coded into the model, resulting in the reasoning ability of large models is superior to humans, but thanks to unsupervised learning and transfer learning, the model can carry out unsupervised learning based on the co-occurrence between words and concepts, at this stage, the model can automatically identify the themes and semantic relationships that exist in it, and at the same time dig out the essential things between the two, such as the civil law system of the civil law the "principle of good faith" and the "implied good faith and fair trade clauses" in common law contract law have the same function and spiritual core, while the expression and source are completely different. On the other hand, transfer learning mechanisms can transfer the "knowledge" or "patterns" that the model has mastered in a certain field to another new field [5]. For example, when a legal practitioner encounters the problem of infringement of AI-generated content, he can also ask LLM to investigate the relevant provisions of the "attachment" system in the real estate law, and try to use the AI model or the prompts and products given by users as a form of expression of the object of rights. From the perspective of institutions, such as the construction of logical thinking such as what kind of rights should be given when AI models are combined with user prompts to create a new thing. The core element is to combine mutually exclusive legal knowledge points into a dynamic and coherent knowledge network, and assist in the establishment of new arguments that can support the argument of new legal disputes. Large language models have a very different paradigm evolution process in legal knowledge generation, and the following is a graphical comparison of different technical implementation paths of legal judgment prediction tasks (Fig. 1).

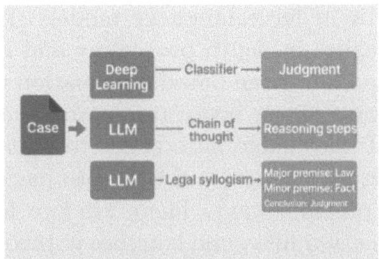

Fig. 1. An overview of three different approaches for Legal Judgment Prediction (LJP): (1) Deep learning text classification models for providing the judgment without any explanations. (2) Chain-of-thought prompting for providing the judgment with intermediate reasoning steps as explanations. (3) Legal syllogism prompting for providing the three deductive reasoning steps: law, fact and judgment

Path (1) is based on the traditional deep learning method, using case facts to directly input and predict the results to the complex classifier model, which may obtain better prediction results in a certain task, but the model has no way of knowing the internal decision-making process, and the model is like a "black box", which will not bring a trustworthy and legally logical reasoning process to legal practitioners, so the application value of this type of method is low [6]. Path (2) is a large-scale language model that uses "chain of thought (CoT)" prompts, that is, adding phrases such as "let's think step by step" can induce the model to give a series of chain information expressing intermediate reasoning, which is conducive to opening the "black box" and enhancing the interpretability of the model [7]. Path (3) is the method that is closer to the thinking of the legal profession, the "Legal Syllogism" prompt method, which directly guides the model to divide the reasoning process into major premises (legal norms), the small premise (case facts) and the conclusion (judgment result). These three structured outputs are closer to the professional thinking habits of legal professionals, making this form of conclusion well understood and recognized by legal practitioners [4]. As can be seen from the figure, large models have promoted legal AI from simple result prediction to process reasoning and knowledge production.

2.2 Counterfactual Exploration and Alternative Framework

After completing the summary of existing knowledge, large-scale language models that generate new knowledge through fusion and transfer also have the ability to create other creative knowledge results, and can envision possibilities that did not exist before, and construct an alternative analysis framework. It is precisely with counterfactual thinking that legal reasoning becomes an objective and reasonable argument, "what would happen if this time/then or so/that/that"; It is based on this that in practice, such as the causal relationship judgment in tort law, such as "If the defendant had not acted, would the damage have occurred?" The foreseeability rule in contract law or the presumption of subjective purpose in criminal law also need to be clarified or judged by such counterfactual inferences. Such a cognitively empirical limited traditional legal analysis cannot exhaust all counterfactual situations. The generation ability of large models is strong, so this method is directly adopted to solve the problem. By providing good instructions, a lawyer can prompt the model to generate numerous alternative opinions, such as diverse legal arguments or defense strategies [1]. For instance, in a complex self-driving car accident case, a lawyer could ask the LLM to generate litigation arguments from the alternative perspectives of aviation accident liability, cybersecurity law, and insurance law. The model can then automatically generate multiple logical and distinct solutions, helping the lawyer to achieve a "legal stress test" for the case. At the same time, because LLMs can take into account more angles, lawyers can also use this to predict other claims that the other party will use and the possible adverse effects, and help overcome one of the cognitive biases, that is, only seeing one-line thinking [8].

However, this ability can be a double-edged sword. The alternative frameworks or counterfactual scenarios generated by the model may be logically inconsistent with legal provisions or lack a factual basis, or may even be based on false factual perceptions or a kind of "illusion" purely fictional [9]. For example, the model may propose to argue a certain point based on abolished laws and regulations, or fabricate an accident situation that cannot happen in reality, which requires us to treat the output of the machine with a professional eye, and see it more as a "tool to stimulate intellectual thinking", rather than directly thinking that this is the answer itself, and it also needs to accept the human brain to judge whether it is reasonable, achievable, or more convincing explanation selected from many possibilities. It can be seen that the function of LLM counterfactual inquiry is to maximize the value of the technical effect in the closed loop of human-machine symbiosis, rather than to promote the outward expansion of thinking [10].

3 Prompt Engineering Technology for Legal Knowledge Generation

To give full play to the knowledge aggregation ability and counterfactual exploration ability of large language models, it is necessary to master the fundamental of their interaction - prompt engineering; Prompt engineering is a series of systematic methods for interaction design, construction, and optimization of large language models, which are used to design, construct, and optimize input instructions (i.e., "prompts") used to prompt language models to obtain the required specific high-quality outputs. Specifically, it is from prompt to answer, including the following two levels of content: one is to construct a good static prompt, and the other is to continuously optimize knowledge by using this interactive and dynamic iterative loop.

3.1 Design Prompts for Human-Machine Collaboration

A good, concise initial prompt is a necessary part of achieving human-robot collaboration. To achieve this goal, it is necessary to translate an open legal task into a series of concrete steps that the model can clearly understand and perform, which contains some important design rules, that is, to form an effective prompting framework [11]. First, any instruction should be specific and accurate, without leaving much room for understanding in the model, and an ambiguous instruction like "analyze this contract" can easily cause the model to return a series of verbose and useless nonsense. In fact, in legal work, most tasks are extremely specific, which means that the tasks are almost accurately measured. Therefore, reasonable and accurate prompts should disassemble the task and use specific and precise verbs to give instructions. For example, the above vague instruction is amended to "Please find all the clauses on the 'limitation of liability' in the contract, and determine whether it is possible to be found invalid in the Civil Code of the People's Republic of China on the grounds that the disposition of the parties' rights and obligations is obviously unfair?" "Clarification will make the search and generation of models targeted [1]".

Secondly, setting the model identity required in a certain scenario can allow the model to mobilize its knowledge and experience in the relevant fields learned in the pre-training materials mentioned above as support, and can stimulate the corresponding thinking mode or behavior habits of such scenarios, for example, the beginning of a sentence can be: "You are an intellectual property lawyer who has been practicing for more than 20 years, so ......" will make the model analyze and reply in a more professional and prudent expression, rather than just a universal chat assistant legal person. Similarly, in specific legal work scenarios, the model can be given corresponding job roles, such as "You are a professional assistant in U.S. federal civil proceedings" [2], and the content generated by the model can automatically align the procedural rules and technical terms in a certain field.

Determining the data, output, and output structure of the final output is the most important step before producing materials, and the next goal can only be achieved by forming measurable indicators first. Users can clearly inform the model how to output content in the prompt, such as "list all evidence and proof objects in the form of a table", "summarize the analysis results according to three key points and the number of words should not exceed 200 words", "write an outline of a legal memorandum in a standard format", etc., so as to ensure that the output results meet the needs of actual work. After clarifying these rules, the model will output in its own way instead of messing around, which also greatly reduces the spam in the output material.

Providing demonstrations is an important way to help the model understand and master the task instances and formats. Demonstration provides a shortcut to the "top-down" of the model, i.e., the demonstration allows the model to make expected responses based on previously seen input-output paradigm imitations. The demonstration allows the model to complete the task without the need for backward transfer and weight adjustment, and can accept new data or task parameters without the need for retraining or tuning [12]. For example, in the case of requesting a production case summary, the model can be provided with a case summary with appropriate content and correct format (or similar model completed work), supplemented by a newly written original case manuscript, and the model can be asked to "write a summary of the following case according to the above paradigm"; However, the demonstration should not be abused, because the demonstration itself will have negative effects - if the quality of the demonstration is low or the demonstration is not in line with the target task enough, it may cause the model to shift the results.

Providing sufficient context and clear clues is an important guarantee for the model to reason in an appropriate range, and the solution of legal problems needs to refer to the specific factual background and legal environment "Anchor" to avoid "hallucinations" or incorrect reasoning caused by lack of sufficient information. Putting the core information required to complete the task into context and providing it to the model is equivalent to artificially realizing a process of "retrieval augmentation generation", that is, artificially obtaining the external knowledge required by the model and supplementing it to the text, and completing the enhanced text output through the model, which can not only make up for the lack or inability to find information from the correct field, but also enhance the accuracy and relevance of the output [13]. For example, the prompt template of the ECHR judgment prediction task completely and clearly contains the facts (context), closed questions (instructions), given options (parameters), and clear answer markers (answers) of the case [14].

3.2 Iterative Prompt-Response Loop for Knowledge Optimization

High-quality starter words are just a good start, and what really matters is the prompt engineering itself, which is based on a dynamic, iterative process of improvement, with an iterative prompt-response cycle (Iterative Prompt-Response Cycle) to continuously promote the continuous refinement and processing of this knowledge. It has evolved from the form of "instruction-execution" to the method of "dialogue-co-creation". The cycle is as follows: first, human experts provide starting prompts according to the above principles and input them into the large model; Then, the model generates a preliminary response; Then, the human expert evaluates the model response, summarizes the advantages and disadvantages of correctness and error, and whether there are omissions or unclearness, and then gives specific feedback information, which may include directly correcting wrong information, asking about confusion, or adding some information that needs to be added to deepen the judgment to achieve the effect of deepening the judgment. Finally, the human expert synthesizes the review information and gives an updated and optimized prompt for the model to instruct and generate again, which is a new cycle.

To illustrate with the help of a contract dispute case, the following process may be undertaken: first, the lawyer puts forward a broader requirement: "find out the potential legal risks from this service agreement", and the model may give some relatively macroscopic risk points; The lawyer will then give feedback and further refine the answer, asking: "The risk points you find are relatively general, can you concentrate on 7.2? In the section "Liability", the content in this section is compared with the latest precedents on Delaware corporate law in the United States", so that the model will give an accurate and more focused and focused answer; In the third round, the lawyer will ask questions about the model's answer, "The conclusion drawn from you is more in-depth, but the other party to this contract dispute is a small start-up technology company with weak financial strength. This iterative process will continue, gradually refine, deepen and condense a problem, and finally use a more operable problem-solving solution that is highly adapted to specific matters as the result of completing the task.

It is a process of "co-creation" between humans and machines [1]. In this process, human experts provide domain knowledge, provide strategic direction, and have critical judgment skills; Large language models leverage their massive knowledge reserves, super pattern discovery capabilities, and efficient generation capabilities. The final result is not a simple replica of human ideas, nor is it an autonomous creation of large models without human guidance, but a new incremental value created by combining the two. Therefore, this also means that for human experts, he has to invest more, not only to have a deep knowledge base in the field to ensure whether he can see the output of large models, but also to give valuable opinions and guidance, which is not something that ordinary professionals can do. If a novice cannot judge the problems of model output, cannot ask targeted questions, and cannot ask ideas, it is likely to fall into a shallow iterative loop and cannot maximize the advantages of large models [15]. Therefore, effective iterative prompting requires human participants to have a high level of expertise and conversation leadership skills.

4   Case Studies: The Application of Prompt Engineering in Legal Practice

In order to apply the various theories of prompt engineering introduced above to the actual situation, a specific problem will be selected to illustrate, and different prompt hierarchies will be used to analyze the different degrees of impact that different prompts can bring to LLMs in a specific case. Its purpose is to intuitively let everyone understand how to implant domain knowledge and standardized instructions into prompts in prompt engineering, so as to transform LLMs into a more intelligent and professional powerful multi-faceted skill collaboration partner.

4.1   Task Definition and Prompt Design: Contract Risk Analysis

For example, in a legal practice scenario, a lawyer needs to conduct a preliminary risk check on a software-as-a-service contract. Party A is the service provider in the contract, mainly to find out the conditions that may be unfavorable to him. Therefore, a reference object is set up here, mainly based on this design to make three gradient-increasing instructions to compare and analyze the strength and weakness of the reminder effect. The complexity level is basic, structured, and professional.

Prompt A (Basic Prompt). The simplest command statement does not tell the model any background information, personas, or results to be achieved.

"Review the following contracts."

Prompt B (Structured Prompt). On the basis of basic prompts, the completeness requirements are added, and on this basis, role-playing and structured output are proposed, so that the model can be analyzed more in an organized manner under reasonable specifications.

"Suppose you are a professional contract review lawyer. Please review the following contracts to identify terms that may pose potential risks to you at the commercial and legal levels. Please present the identified risk points in a list and attach a brief explanation of the reasons for each risk point".

Prompt C (Advanced Prompt). On the basis of the original structured prompts, senior professional roles are added, and a special legal analysis framework (legal syllogism) is embedded in the problem description to decompose the task more specifically [16]. This change is intended to improve the model's ability to extract knowledge points and promote the model to deepen its reasoning cognition on this problem.

> "You are a top commercial lawyer with over 15 years of experience negotiating complex contracts in the technology sector. Use the analytical framework of the 'legal syllogism' to conduct an in-depth analysis of the two core clauses of 'Limitation of Liability' and 'Intellectual Property Ownership' in the attached SaaS service contract. For each clause, your analysis must include the following three parts:
> - **Major premise:** Interpret the general legal principles or normal business practices or mandatory legal provisions involved in this paragraph.
> - **Minor premise:** Accurately quote the text of specific terms in the contract.
> - **Conclusion:** Based on the content of the major premise and the minor premise, we judge whether this clause constitutes a specific risk and the corresponding risk level (high/medium/low) for us as a service provider, and put forward specific suggestions for improvement of the terms of this contract."

The design of these three prompts is the result of the gradual refinement of the prompt vector, which gradually improves the accuracy of the instructions, expands the context, and enhances the professional analysis framework. It is used to explore whether prompt engineering technology has a significant effect on improving the output quality of LLMs.

4.2 Comparative Analysis of LLM-Generated Content and Human Expert Review

In terms of the three different prompts given above, the quality of the articles produced by large language models represented by GPT-4 is very different, which is the most direct example of how the quality of the prompt is closely related to the generated results.

Response to Prompt A. The output from Basic Prompt A was overly general and lacked practical value.

Response to Prompt B. With the help of character design and structured instructions, the model's output quality improved. Structured Prompt B, while able to identify initial risks, lacked analytical depth and failed to provide specific solutions.

Response to Prompt C. Because the C prompt has the highest precision, a professional framework, and a focused task, the model's output was the best. Advanced Prompt C, by guiding the model to use the 'legal syllogism' framework, successfully proceeded from legal and business practices (major premise), combined them with specific contract clauses (minor premise), and arrived at an in-depth risk assessment with concrete suggestions for amendment (conclusion).

From the perspective of an experienced lawyer as an evaluator, it can be judged that the effect of prompt A is very poor and has almost no useful value in actual work; The effect of prompt B is to provide a rough risk identification list, but it lacks the depth and breadth of analysis, does not meet the requirements of the standard, and needs to be supplemented and improved. Relatively speaking, the output effect of prompt C is very good, it is very clear about the entire logical structure, and every detail has sufficient basis, and the accuracy of each possible risk is accurately studied and judged, and specific modification suggestions are given for each result, and even specific executable suggestions are given [10]. This output can be directly used as a lawyer's work paper, which saves a lot of time and energy to do this at once. This case study serves as a powerful example of how prompt engineering can be a critical variable in determining the success or failure of LLM applications in the legal field. A well-designed prompt that maximizes the potential of the model and produces knowledge that meets professional standards [17].

4.3 Insights and Limitations Found in Practical Application

Through the above cases, we can extract some experience summaries about the use of prompt engineering in legal practice, and of course, we must also make it clear that prompt engineering has its own defects and shortcomings that cannot be ignored. The first important conclusion is to integrate domain knowledge explicitly into prompt design, which is to improve LLMsThe best path in the ability to complete professional tasks. In the example given above, letting the model directly "review the contract" is far less than guiding the model to use the "legal syllogism" to think of legal people. Therefore, we can see that in fact, effective prompt engineering is not a kind of semantic engineering, and the most important thing for prompt engineering is that the user himself also needs to have a certain knowledge base in the field to disassemble a more complex professional thinking process into some specific steps that can be understood and executed by the model [4]. The second important finding is that splitting a large task into several specific, small, and manageable subtasks can effectively increase the quality and relevance of the output, because prompt C does not leave the task of reviewing the entire contract to the model, but only lets it pay attention to the two most important clauses, which is actually a "divide and conquer" method, which can help the model better allocate its "attention" and make deeper judgments, instead of just tasting it [18].

However, despite this, the good responses generated from C-level prompts are not perfect, and their flaws reflect the boundaries that existing LLMs may have, for example, in the process of LLM parsing the "limitation of liability" clause, it is not specific to a specific itemSaaS application scenario, which is not in line with the facts. In the case of the company's system in this case, the software developed by the company to process data that is more sensitive and protected by specific laws (such as HIPAA in the United States). This means that the specific amount given by the model for the above limits may be considered invalid due to the relevant provisions applied by the system itself or the mandatory provisions of laws and regulations. In addition to the above-mentioned lack of understanding of a specific fact or commercial situation, the model will also quote an authoritative law and regulation (such as the Civil Code) under normal circumstances because it does not dare to take the liberty when invoking the "major premise" Taking one of these provisions too hastily, or creating a non-existent judicial interpretation, or far-fetching a legal document that has expired, is an act of creating an "illusion" and creating a dangerous legal risk to the audience that seems correct but is actually a serious error [9].

The advantages of the above technologies/platforms as examples fully illustrate that the disadvantages brought by artificial intelligence to legal work will eventually lead to the conclusion that the judgment, decision-making and final responsibility of human experts are essential in all legal work with the help of artificial intelligence. Even if LLMs can be like a well-trained and extremely capable "co-pilot", they can handle things efficiently and accurately, and give various possible paths. But the ultimate goal is to sit in the cockpit, be responsible for the final driving decision, always pay attention to the weather conditions (any accidents or legal issues), and ensure the smooth operation of the whole work, that is, the "captain", that is, the human lawyer [1]. This case also shows well that the production of legal knowledge is actually a process of deep integration between man and machine, artificial intelligence to gain humans, assist humans, and cannot replace the human brain, and the key ability of legal professionals in the future is not to use an advanced robot, but to use an effective dialogue and communication mechanism to make large robots work for me, make good use of dialogue and communication to enhance human intelligence, and also help to create better results [19].

5   Key Challenges and Ethical Considerations

In the process of enabling the generation of legal knowledge, large language models need to be very cautious due to their own technical limitations and a series of ethical issues. This is mainly done through data, algorithms, applications, and corresponding responsibilities. For such technology, we can only make the best use of the benefits it brings, and we must treat it with a high degree of critical awareness. Otherwise, LLMs will not be able to contribute to the quality of legal services, and may even damage the fairness and professionalism of the law.

5.1   The Problem of "Hallucination" and the Need for Fact-Checking

One of the inherent problems inherent in technically the most maligned large-scale language models is "hallucinations". Hallucinations are when the content generated by the model may fabricate information that seems reasonable but is actually completely contrary to reality [9]. This issue arises because LLMs are designed to predict the next word in a sequence based on statistical patterns, rather than verifying facts, which can lead them to "create" plausible-sounding but false information [9]. As a specific professional field that emphasizes the truth of facts and the authenticity of law, the harm of "hallucinations" is quite fatal in this link that requires extremely high accuracy. A so-called authoritative, unquestionable legal argument derived from LLM is likely to be based on a false precedent, an abolished law, or even a false case fact. Recently, there are real precedents showing that lawyers were severely disciplined for bringing documents provided by platforms such as ChatGPT containing false precedent citations into the court for submission [1].

Therefore, attention should be paid to the key way to solve the problem of "illusion", that is, the whole chain of strict prevention of man-machine cooperation fact-verification. "Never trust completely, always keep checking" is the creed that all lawyers using LLMs should abide by, according to these three points one by one, that is, a comprehensive response is formed, and it is also in accordance with the beforehand, During and after the event, it is necessary to select some specialized legal AI tools that not only have real-time networking search functions but also can connect to reliable legal database API interfaces, and use RAG technology to bind the model's generation capabilities to reliable knowledge. Fundamentally reduce the possibility of hallucinations in the model [13]. The second step is to use prompts to control the behavior of the model, such as telling the model that "each legal argument must provide a corresponding case number or law article number", or asking it to explain that "if one of the following facts is adopted, the page number and paragraph of the part of the content are as follows". The last step, and the best step to ensure quality, is to manually review the results provided by the model, especially key elements such as precedents, laws, data, and core facts need to be manually reviewed, and then manually checked, requiring people to use authoritative databases such as Westlaw and LexisNexis to review the reasons Whether the AI-generated content is correct.

5.2 Inherent Bias in Legal Data and the Risk of Amplifying Inequality

A large amount of corpus knowledge and "worldview" are learned from massive data by large language models, and in the process, they will unreservedly absorb historically existing and systematic social biases, and this prejudice will also subtly affect the subsequent creation process, which may in turn expand and solidify social prejudices that were originally very understated or unnoticed [20]. Legal data, with its long history of judgments reflecting past societal power structures and prejudices, contains inherent biases regarding factors like gender, race, and social class [20]. If an LLM can be trained with access to such historical data, it may learn and adopt factual connections between certain groups and negative labels such as "high risk", "untrustworthy", and "guilty" during the creation process. This internalized bias may also pose a risk of serious social injustice when applied to the legal field. Assuming that there is an LLM applied to the criminal justice field to assist judges in making corresponding opinions on bail and sentencing, and the LLM's training corpus contains bias against a certain group, it may put defendants with similar backgrounds at a disadvantage in sentencing due to their racial issues. In the civil field, there is an AI resume screening application, which may automatically classify female candidates in the corresponding position because it has learned that the proportion of subordinate groups occupying a certain position in the past is too large (e.g., male). This kind of algorithmic bias is cloaked in the cloak of "objective" and "neutral", which is more likely to appear hidden than human bias, and is less likely to be detected and challenged, and will also damage the basic requirements of equality in the rule of law [21].

Dealing with algorithmic bias is a series of systematic work that needs to be continuously improved. The first is to conduct strict audit and cleaning of the trained data in the model development stage, and try to eliminate the biased data in it. In addition, more and more advanced algorithmic fairness technologies should be developed, so that the model can discover and reduce the impact of bias in the data during the training process [22]. The second is that the application side can be assisted by prompt engineering technology: the user of the prompt can self-consistently add instructions to the prompt to resist bias, for example, "When doing risk assessment, please be completely based on the objective facts provided, and do not have stereotypes such as race, gender, social status", but the method of the prompt side has a certain limit. Biases hidden deep within the model are difficult to completely eliminate with one or two simple anti-bias instructions. A more preferable approach is to set up a dedicated post-processing bias detection and correction tool for LLMs to scan the LLM's output results and identify possible biases, and mark human users with an alert flag to remind humans to review and correct. Finally, the more about human rights and freedoms, the more high-risk events must be adhered to the principle of "meaningful human control", that is, our algorithms can only play an auxiliary role, not make decisive judgments.

5.3 Professional Responsibility and the Ethics of Artificial Intelligence-Assisted Legal Work

The application of large models to legal practice will have a huge impact on the professional ethics of traditional lawyers, testing some basic issues, mainly the confidentiality of clients, the ability and diligence of lawyers, and the assumption of legal responsibility. The foundation of the lawyer's profession is to keep clients confidential, and if lawyers use publicly available, consumer-grade LLM services, there are very large risks to data security and privacy [23]. Since the privacy policy of most of these services explicitly mentions, users will treat the user's input as data that is subsequently provided to the model for training or analysis. Therefore, when lawyers upload their clients' sensitive cases, trade secrets, personal information and other documents to such platforms, it is equivalent to exposing the client's information to the uncontrollable and unstable third-party network environment, which is a serious violation of the lawyer's confidentiality obligations to the client. Therefore, responsible law firms or legal departments must establish effective AI usage policies, prohibiting the use of unvetted public tools. They should prioritize private deployments or sign strict DPAs with enterprise-level providers to ensure data protection and confidentiality [24].

The ability and duty of diligence of lawyers have been given new meaning in the era of AI. In the past, the so-called "ability" was the corresponding legal knowledge and legal skills of the lawyer, but now the "ability" includes the most basic "technical ability", that is, knowing what the technical tool we use, what its principle is, what kind of scope of use it is, and what are the inherent risks in the process [25]. Experienced lawyers are able to determine when LLMs can be used help to realize the facts of the case or the results of the conversation record more accurately, and they will have a certain degree of speculation about the results. It is undeniable that if you rely on boldness and without review, you will directly use the think tank of DJI aircraft carrier products, which is undoubtedly a very stupid performance. In addition, the duty of diligence is manifested in the fact that as a lawyer, you must devote sufficient time and energy to professional activities, think about problems, ascertain facts, review evidence, analyze arguments, etc., and cannot leave it to AI to make decisions. Otherwise, the professionalism of the lawyer will be lost, and the quality of service to clients will be affected from the source.

The so-called "responsibility issue" is actually another major problem in AI legal assistance work in addition to the above-mentioned ethical dilemma, that is, when LLMs are deeply involved in the drafting and production of legal strategies, contract terms, pleadings and other documents, causing adverse consequences to customers, then who should bear the risk: First, the information error is due to Is it caused by the wrong information entered by the AI model developer? Or is it caused by a design flaw in the AI algorithm? Second, who failed to find these defects, the person involved or the lawyer? Or did it condone the law firm that condoned the launch and use of the problematic AI software? All in all, the existing legal responsibility system does not give an answer to this, and in this case, it will inevitably cause people to build a new system in this regard [26]. Therefore, the author envisions taking the strengthening of "law" as an example, strengthening lawyers as the "producers" of the final product, and lawyers should be fully responsible for any work results, rather than "AI mistakes". Then the association and regulatory authorities should promptly issue best practices and codes of conduct on how to use AI responsibly in legal practice, which is useful to lawyers and the industry, and even foreseeable that there will be relevant legal disputes in the future.

6 Conclusion

Under its influence, legal artificial intelligence no longer stays at the level of simple retrieval of rules and knowledge bases or auxiliary analysis to help people complete their work, but moves towards a new era where it can truly create new knowledge for itself and work with human peers to discover and produce new knowledge. Firstly, the use of detailed prompts designed according to the framework of legal expertise can prompt large language models to integrate and analogize information across the knowledge boundaries of different fields, and complete innovative reasoning tasks in the case of creating new counterfactuals. Secondly, injecting legal syllogisms and other specialized analysis modes into the large model can make the generated legal documents not only have high accuracy, but also have high interpretability and practicality, and greatly improve the quality of human-machine collaboration.

However, this technical prospect is tied to the flaws of the model itself and the deep ethical challenges. On the one hand, "illusion" requires legal professionals to adhere to the principle of seeking truth from facts and be inviolable; On the other hand, the social bias hidden behind the training data will be further amplified under the influence of algorithms, bringing potential threats to legal fairness and justice. On the other hand, the AI era has brought new issues such as client confidentiality, lawyer ability, and lawyer responsibility, and has put forward more stringent requirements for new legal professional ethics.

In this regard, the next step in legal knowledge generation should focus on building a human-centered Deep-Cogitative Human-Machine Synergy model [27], through methods such as AI The Humans partnership is collaboratively constructed, using artificial intelligence as a powerful tool to assist the human brain, and using it to assist human lawyers in a way that allows them to maintain the ultimate critical thinking and the ability to make value judgments and ethical responsibilities. In the future, an important part of lawyers' core value is that legal talents act as prudent "system operators" and ultimate "responsibility bearers" to correctly lead technology towards the goal of the rule of law [28,29].

References

1. Regalia, J.: From briefs to bytes: how generative AI is transforming legal writing and practice. Tulsa L. Rev. **59**, 193 (2024)
2. Krumov, K., Boytcheva, S., Koytchev, I.: SU-FMI at SemEval-2024 task 5: from BERT fine-tuning to LLM prompt engineering-approaches in legal argument reasoning. In: Proceedings of the 18th International Workshop on Semantic Evaluation (SemEval-2024) (2024)
3. Marvin, G., et al.: Prompt engineering in large language models. In: International Conference on Data Intelligence and Cognitive Informatics. Springer, Singapore (2023)
4. Jiang, C., Yang, X.: Legal syllogism prompting: Teaching large language models for legal judgment prediction. In: Proceedings of the Nineteenth International Conference on Artificial Intelligence and Law (2023)
5. Liu, P., et al.: Pre-train, prompt, and predict: a systematic survey of prompting methods in natural language processing. ACM Comput. Surv. **55**(9), 1–35 (2023)
6. Feng, Y., Li, C., Ng, V.: Legal judgment prediction: a survey of the state of the art. In: IJCAI, pp. 5461–5469 (2022)

7. Wei, J., et al.: Chain-of-thought prompting elicits reasoning in large language models. Adv. Neural. Inf. Process. Syst. **35**, 24824–24837 (2022)
8. Hagendorff, T., Fabi, S., Kosinski, M.: Human-like intuitive behavior and reasoning biases emerged in large language models but disappeared in chatgpt. Nat. Comput. Sci. **3**(10), 833–838 (2023)
9. Huang, L., et al.: A survey on hallucination in large language models: principles, taxonomy, challenges, and open questions. ACM Trans. Inf. Syst. **43**(2), 1–55 (2025)
10. Dell'Acqua, F., et al.: Navigating the jagged technological frontier: field experimental evidence of the effects of AI on knowledge worker productivity and quality. Harvard Business School Technology & Operations Mgt. Unit Working Paper 24-013 (2023)
11. Bsharat, S.M., Myrzakhan, A., Shen, Z.: Principled instructions are all you need for questioning llama-1/2, GPT-3.5/4. arXiv preprint arXiv:2312.16171 (2023)
12. Mann, B., et al.: Language models are few-shot learners. arXiv preprint arXiv:2005.14165, vol. 1, no. 3, p. 3 (2020)
13. Gao, Y., et al.: Retrieval-augmented generation for large language models: a survey. arXiv preprint arXiv:2312.10997, vol. 2, no. 1 (2023)
14. Trautmann, D., Petrova, A., Schilder, F.: Legal prompt engineering for multilingual legal judgement prediction. arXiv preprint arXiv:2212.02199 (2022)
15. Zanzotto, F.M.: Human-in-the-loop artificial intelligence. J. Artif. Intell. Res. **64**, 243–252 (2019)
16. Cheng, Z., et al.: Binding language models in symbolic languages. arXiv preprint arXiv:2210.02875 (2022)
17. Zamfirescu-Pereira, J.D., et al.: Why Johnny can't prompt: how non-AI experts try (and fail) to design LLM prompts. In: Proceedings of the 2023 CHI Conference on Human Factors in Computing Systems (2023)
18. Wang, W., et al.: Layout and task aware instruction prompt for zero-shot document image question answering. arXiv preprint arXiv:2306.00526 (2023)
19. Daugherty, P.R., Wilson, H.J.: Human+ Machine, Updated and Expanded. Reimagining Work in the Age of AI. Harvard Business Press (2024)
20. Barocas, S., Selbst, A.D.: Big data's disparate impact. Calif. L. Rev. **104**, 671 (2016)
21. Eubanks, V.: Automating inequality: how high-tech tools profile, police, and punish the poor. St. Martin's Press (2018)
22. Mehrabi, N., et al.: A survey on bias and fairness in machine learning. ACM Comput. Surv. (CSUR) **54**(6), 1–35 (2021)
23. OpenAI: Privacy Policy. OpenAI Policies (2024)
24. American Bar Association (ABA) Formal Opinion 498, "Virtual Practice" (2021)
25. American Bar Association (ABA), Model Rules of Professional Conduct, Rule 1.1, Comment 8 (2012, revised)
26. Baş, F.: Artificial intelligence, human and society in the context of ulrich beck's risk society theory. Eskişehir Osmangazi Üniversitesi İlahiyat Fakültesi Dergisi **12**, 43–59 (2025)
27. Kumar, S., et al.: Applications, challenges, and future directions of human-in-the-loop learning. IEEE Access **12**, 75735–75760 (2024)
28. Terzidou, K.: Generative AI for the legal profession: Facing the implications of the use of ChatGPT through an intradisciplinary approach. MediaLaws (2023)
29. Dey, S., Das, A.: Robotic process automation: assessment of the technology for transformation of business processes. Int. J. Bus. Process. Integr. Manag. **9**(3), 220–230 (2019)

A Review of Privacy Protection in the News Industry Driven by Artificial Intelligence Technologies

Jingbo Gao[1,2], Shahrul Nazmi Sannusi[1(✉)], Jamaluddin Aziz[1], and Qi Liang[3]

[1] Universiti Kebangsaan Malaysia, Bangi, Malaysia
nazmy@ukm.edu.my
[2] Chongqing Normal University, Chongqing 401331, China
[3] Communication University of China, Beijing 100024, China

Abstract. Artificial intelligence (AI) technologies have enhanced operational efficiency and personalized services in news through content generation, distribution, and user behavior analysis. However, they introduce privacy risks like unauthorized data collection across the data lifecycle. Meanwhile, the industry faces dual challenges from technological implementation complexities and lagging legal-ethical frameworks. This survey systematically reviews AI-driven privacy protection in news, outlining application scenarios, privacy risks, and technical, legal-ethical solutions (e.g., federated learning, differential privacy). By synthesizing existing research contributions and identifying gaps, this work proposes future research directions in technical optimization, legal framework enhancement, and social ethics construction, providing a comprehensive reference for the field's advancement.

Keywords: News Industry Privacy · News Recommendation Systems · Cross-border News Data Flow · Differential Privacy · Federated Learning

1 Introduction

Artificial intelligence (AI) has transformed the news industry, enabling real-time content generation (e.g., Tencent's "Dream Writer") and personalized filtering via deep learning user profiles [1, 2]. However, this brings privacy risks: unauthorized data collection (e.g., browsing trajectories) and sensitive inference from non-sensitive data. The industry faces dual challenges: technical complexities (e.g., balancing data utility and privacy) and lagging legal-ethical frameworks for AI-specific risks like cross-border flows.

Existing research has some limitations. In terms of adversarial attacks and defense, under the federated learning framework, gradient inversion attacks pose a risk of reconstructing users' private information from news data, yet current defense strategies are insufficiently adapted to the unstructured nature of news text. High computational overheads associated with encryption techniques [26], the "privacy-utility" trade-off challenge of differential privacy, and the lack of defenses against cross-platform attacks and dynamic attack evolution are all issues.

Lagging ethics and legal regulations are also a problem. Analysis of 57 policy documents from 24 countries shows ethical and legal frameworks lag in adapting to journalism's specific AI scenarios. Emerging issues such as excessive personal data collection by automated news gathering technologies and privacy preference misuse caused by algorithmic recommendations have yet to form systematic ethical consensus or legal constraints [17].

At the level of explainability and transparency, the "black box" nature of algorithms makes it difficult to effectively identify and assess privacy risks [28]. In practical applications within the news industry, there is a lack of customized solutions for privacy protection, and a lack of transparency mechanisms at the interaction level between news organizations and users.

The study uses interdisciplinary methods, integrating theories from communication, law, and computer science. In the research of technical privacy protection means, it analyzes technologies such as data encryption [12], differential privacy [26], federated learning, and homomorphic encryption [27], using cases like federated learning for browsing history protection and differential privacy for behavior report publishing.

In terms of legal and ethical norm research, based on laws and regulations such as the EU's General Data Protection Regulation (GDPR) [18] and China's Personal Information Protection Law [19], combined with the principles of journalism ethics [21], it analyzes regulatory challenges like cross-border data flow, algorithmic transparency, and AI liability determination.

This survey makes several contributions. It systematically reviews AI-driven privacy protection in the news industry, outlining application scenarios, privacy risks, and technical, legal-ethical solutions. These solutions include technologies like federated learning: a Distributed Machine Learning framework where 'data remains stationary while the model moves' [11, 16] and differential privacy: a technique that adds random noise to data to ensure individual privacy while allowing statistical analysis [26]. By synthesizing existing research contributions and identifying gaps, the work provides a comprehensive reference for the field's advancement.

This paper conducts a systematic discussion around the privacy protection issues in the news field driven by artificial intelligence technology. Section 2 provides an overview of the applications of artificial intelligence technology in the news field and privacy risks. Section 3 introduces the technical means of privacy protection in the news field. Section 4 introduces the legal framework and ethical challenges of privacy protection in the news field. Section 5 summarizes the existing research progress and key deficiencies. Section 6 looks forward to the development direction of privacy protection in the news field from three dimensions: the technical level, the legal level, and the social and ethical level. Section 7 concludes the paper.

2 AI in News: Applications, Privacy Risks, and Protection Technologies

2.1 Application of Artificial Intelligence Technology in the News Field

News Content Generation and Distribution

Against the backdrop of today's digital era, artificial intelligence (AI) technology is profoundly transforming the news industry, demonstrating tremendous potential and influence in the areas of news content generation and distribution.

AI-driven news production has revolutionized content creation, significantly enhancing operational efficiency and reducing labor costs [1].

In terms of content generation, AI technology exhibits strong capabilities in personalized recommendations. Based on big data analysis, it can accurately identify user interests and preferences. By collecting data such as users' browsing history, search records, and dwell time on news platforms, the system can construct detailed user profiling and deliver suitable content to users at the appropriate time and location.

AI optimizes news distribution via personalized recommendation and information filtering. During the evaluation phase, AI facilitates the construction of a comprehensive evaluation system incorporating classical metrics along with indicators such as diversity and novelty, thereby holistically measuring the effectiveness of recommendations [1]. These strategies dynamically capture user interest preferences using machine learning and deep learning algorithms.

User Behavior Analysis and Profiling

With the vigorous development of artificial intelligence technology, user behavior analysis and profiling have become critical components of personalized news services, yet they also pose unprecedented challenges to privacy protection.

At the level of user behavior analysis, artificial intelligence achieves precise user behavior insights through multi-dimensional data collection and analysis. News platforms employ AI to fuse explicit data (e.g., reading duration, clickstream) and implicit data (e.g., comment sentiment analyzed via natural language processing) for dynamic user profiling. For example, one study applied a deep learning model to analyze users' interaction patterns with different types of news and achieved an 88% accuracy rate in predicting users' political inclinations, demonstrating the powerful capabilities of AI in behavioral analysis [4].

AI constructs fine-grained user profiles via machine learning (e.g., collaborative filtering), updating interest tags in real-time. A study developed a deep learning model that, relying solely on users' abstract browsing history, could effectively predict their research interests. This dynamic profiling capability enables news platforms to deliver personalized content recommendations and enhance user engagement [5].

2.2 Analysis of Privacy Leakage Risks in the News Industry

Figure 1 highlights the potential privacy risks that may exist in each stage of the news process. In the following text, we will also provide detailed explanations of the security risks at each stage.

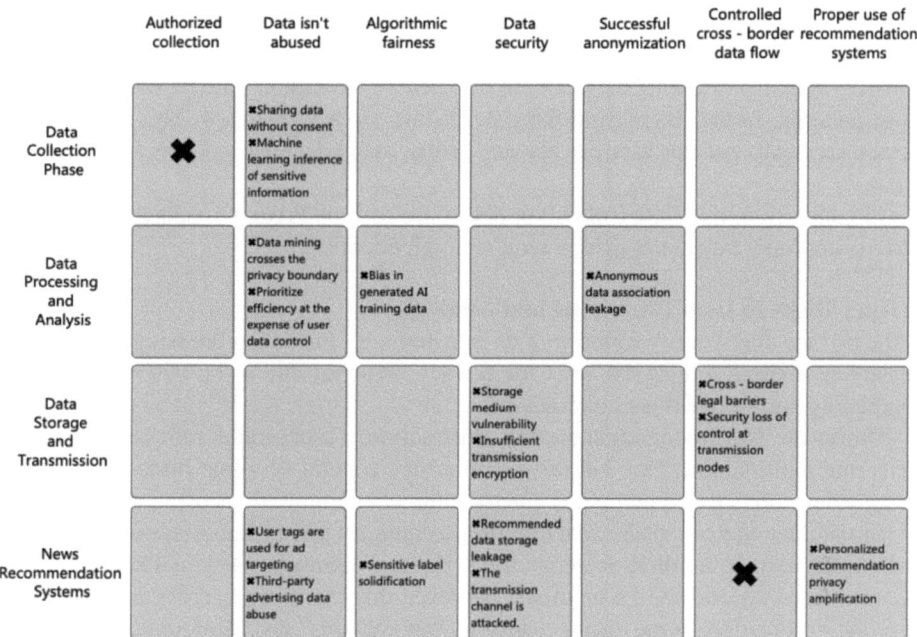

Fig. 1. News industry data Privacy Risks map

Privacy Risks in the Data Collection Phase

In today's digital information era, the news industry has achieved rapid development through the application of artificial intelligence technologies, providing users with personalized news content. Behind this advancement, data collection has become a key pillar supporting intelligent development in the news field. News platforms collect various types of user data to gain deep insights into user needs, thereby enabling precise content delivery and personalized services. However, this process harbors numerous privacy risks.

As AI expands in news, data collection scales up, and unauthorized data harvesting has become rampant. Unauthorized data collection remains a critical risk, with platforms often harvesting user data (e.g., reading habits, interests) without explicit consent or transparent notification [6]. This practice is exacerbated by data brokerage models, where user data is shared with third-party advertisers for targeted marketing, as observed in both social media (e.g., Facebook) and news sectors [7]. Unauthorized data collection infringes user privacy rights, enabling targeted advertising abuse and privacy breaches. These data may also be illegally sold, leading to users becoming victims of fraud, which poses a direct threat to their property safety [6].

At the same time, because users often click to agree without carefully reading the terms of online service contracts, platforms such as Facebook and Google take advantage of this situation by collecting and freely selling the information submitted by users to other companies [7]. In the news industry, some news platforms exhibit similar behavior—they share collected user data with third-party advertisers, who use this data for targeted ad placements, significantly disrupting users' normal news browsing experience. Moreover, machine learning techniques can infer sensitive information from non-sensitive data; for example, they can predict a user's emotional state based on keyboard input patterns, further increasing the risk of data privacy breaches. This kind of data misuse seriously violates user privacy and brings many negative impacts to users' lives [7].

In conclusion, the Data Collection phase has serious Privacy Leakage Risk due to various improper behaviors, which requires high attention.

Privacy Risks in Data Processing and Analysis
In the privacy and security framework of data domains, the data processing and analysis phase has become a high-risk area for privacy breaches due to its inherent technical complexity and frequent data interactions.

During the data processing stage, the construction of user profiles relies on algorithms analyzing multi-source data, but this process may contain systemic biases. Generative AI may develop biased stereotypes due to training data limitations [8].

In the data analysis phase, data mining techniques are an important means. These techniques extract implicit patterns from massive datasets using association rules, machine learning, and similar methods. However, this process may cross the boundaries of privacy protection. Some data that appears "anonymous" may, after multidimensional association analysis, reveal sensitive information [2].

These risks stem from the "efficiency-privacy" contradiction in data processing. The core objective of generative AI and data mining technologies is to maximize data value, but this process often comes at the expense of users' control over their data. On one hand, users lack both awareness of and choice regarding data processing rules; on the other hand, the technical complexity makes it difficult for regulators to effectively assess the fairness and safety of algorithms [8].

Privacy Risks in Data Storage and Transmission
Data storage and transmission are high-risk stages in the privacy lifecycle. AI systems' reliance on data exposes vulnerabilities like storage media flaws or configuration gaps. For example, some AI companies, in pursuit of data processing efficiency, fail to regularly update security patches for storage systems, allowing hackers to exploit known vulnerabilities, gain unauthorized access to servers, and steal sensitive information [9]. Second, when data is transmitted across networks without end-to-end encryption or with insufficient encryption strength, it becomes highly susceptible to interception via man-in-the-middle attacks. Thirdly, due to fundamental differences between AI system algorithms and human cognition, "latent risks" may emerge during data storage and processing.

Secondly, driven by global business expansion and the demand for data mobility, cross-border data transfers have become an international challenge in privacy protection. First, significant legal barriers exist for cross-border compliance. Different countries and regions exhibit notable discrepancies in legislation regarding data sovereignty and privacy protection. Second, there is a risk of losing control over security in the transmission link. Cross-border data transmission typically passes through network nodes governed by multiple jurisdictions, and each node could potentially become a point of privacy leakage. Third, regulatory coordination faces practical challenges. Disputes involving cross-border data often require jurisdictional coordination among law enforcement agencies from different countries, yet the international community has not yet established a unified mechanism for privacy enforcement cooperation. Once a data breach involves multiple countries, the legal remedies and compensation standards across these nations are difficult to effectively align, allowing companies to exploit regulatory gaps and evade responsibility.

Privacy Challenges in News Recommendation Systems
In the ecosystem of news recommendation systems, the tension between user profiling and personalized recommendations permeates the entire chain including data collection, model training, and recommendation execution.

Personalized recommendation relies on precise matching between user profiles and news content, but this process can act as an "amplifier" for privacy leakage. Models like DKN utilize knowledge graphs to associate entities from news clicked by users with knowledge bases, thereby constructing personalized recommendation logic. However, when users frequently browse news involving sensitive topics such as race or religion, these tags might be algorithmically solidified as "long-term interests" and used to offer targeted advertising services to advertisers, resulting in unintentional privacy leakage of users' preference information [10].

Security vulnerabilities during the storage and transmission of user profiling data provide practical pathways for privacy leakage. Under centralized storage architectures, Adressa once experienced a server security breach that led to the exposure of millions of users' click records, including sensitive browsing histories traceable to individual identities. Even with distributed architectures such as federated learning, communication channels between clients and servers remain susceptible to attacks [11].

The contradiction between user profiling and personalized recommendations essentially reflects a value conflict in the digital era between "service precision" and "privacy autonomy." For news recommendation systems to achieve sustainable development, they must go beyond the logic of "efficiency first" by incorporating privacy protection into the foundational architecture of algorithm design. This would enable users to enjoy the convenience of information while maintaining control over their personal privacy data.

2.3 Privacy Protection Technologies and Methods in the News Field Driven by Artificial Intelligence

Technical Privacy Protection Measures
Regarding the issue of privacy protection in the field of journalism, currently there are two main methods: data encryption and homomorphic encryption.

Throughout the entire lifecycle of news data, security during data transmission and storage constitutes key aspects of privacy protection, and data encryption serves as an important technical means to achieve this objective. Data encryption encodes data, transforming plaintext into ciphertext, thereby making it difficult for attackers to interpret the information even if they illegally obtain the data during transmission or storage. During the process of transmitting news data—whether from news collection devices to editing systems or from servers to user terminals—encryption technology prevents data from being stolen. Regarding data storage, encrypting sensitive information in news databases, such as users' browsing records and personal identification information, effectively prevents unauthorized access. For example, using the AES algorithm to encrypt data ensures that only authorized personnel with the correct decryption key can access the data, thus protecting the privacy of news data during storage [12].

Homomorphic encryption enables computation on encrypted data, preserving privacy while enabling data utility. In the news industry, when analysis needs to be performed on encrypted news data, homomorphic encryption demonstrates its unique advantages. For example, homomorphic encryption allows encrypted news data (e.g., click counts, comments) to be analyzed directly without decryption. This way, throughout the entire analysis process, the news data remains encrypted at all times, effectively protecting data privacy while simultaneously meeting the needs of news organizations for data analysis and processing [13].

In summary, technical approaches such as data encryption and homomorphic encryption provide strong support from different perspectives for privacy protection in the AI-driven news industry, helping promote the healthy development of the news sector under the premise of safeguarding user privacy.

Key Technology Analysis
With the vigorous development of Artificial Intelligence, privacy protection issues in the news field are becoming increasingly prominent. A series of advanced technologies have emerged, firmly strengthening the privacy protection for the news industry. The following will focus on the application of differential privacy and federated learning in this field.

The application of differential privacy in news recommendation.

Differential privacy, as a Privacy Protection framework with a rigorous mathematical definition and relatively low computational overhead, plays an important role in the field of news recommendation. In the News Recommendation System, Matrix Factorization is a classic technique for achieving Personalized Recommendation. It Precise Push Notification content by mining the potential associations between users and news content. However, there is a significant Privacy Leakage Risk in the process of utilizing massive user data. To address this issue, researchers have introduced differential privacy into such systems [14]. This technology hides individuals' Sensitive Information by adding Random Noise to the data, and demonstrates its key value when analyzing users' browsing Behavioral Data for Personalized Recommendation in the news field. Taking the matrix factorization recommendation model based on Adaptive Gaussian Differential Privacy (Adaptive Differential Privacy Matrix Factorization) as an example, it designs two effective methods, Adaptive Clipping and adaptive noise adjustment, in the Model Training phase: Adaptive Clipping dynamically determines the clipping threshold for the current training based on the average L2 norm of the Gradients of the item factor vectors in the previous round, which not only avoids Gradients explosion but also reduces the model instability caused by a fixed threshold; adaptive noise adjustment reasonably adjusts the noise scale according to the change in the model's prediction accuracy, improving the recommendation performance while ensuring the Privacy Protection level. Through these measures, Adaptive Differential Privacy Matrix Factorization provides users with high - precision news recommendations and implements differential Privacy Protection on their implicit feedback data, effectively balancing the recommendation accuracy and Privacy Security [15].

The application of federated learning in news recommendation.

Federated learning (FL), as a Distributed Machine Learning paradigm, supports multiple clients in collaboratively training models while ensuring that the original data remains local. Its core principle of "data stays put while the model moves" enables News Platform to complete training without sharing sensitive user Behavioral Data, simply by aggregating model Gradients or parameters. This advantage is fully demonstrated in Privacy Protection-oriented recommendation scenarios [11, 16].

In the field of news recommendation, different institutions often possess unique User Interaction data, but privacy concerns hinder the direct sharing of this data. With the help of federated learning, each platform can train recommendation models using local data, then upload Model Parameters or Gradients to the Central Server for aggregation, ultimately forming a globally optimized recommendation model [11].

The application of federated learning in traditional news recommendation.

In the traditional news recommendation model, the centralized storage and processing of massive User Browsing History not only pose Data Leakage Risk, but the large volume of data transmission also reduces the efficiency of real-time recommendation [16]. After applying federated learning, each client can train the recommendation model locally (e.g., using the GRU network to capture users' short-term interests and combining linear and non-linear features for scoring), and then upload the Gradients updates to the server. The server aggregates these updates to iteratively optimize the Global Model, and then distributes the optimized model back to each client.

For example, News Organizations in different regions can train the Personalized Recommendation model based on local user click data, and collaboratively improve the recommendation accuracy through the federated learning framework. On datasets such as Adressa and MIND, indicators such as AUC and nDCG have been significantly improved. At the same time, the transmission of original browsing records across institutions is avoided, maximizing the protection of Privacy Security. This model of "model migration replacing data migration" not only breaks down data barriers but also takes into account both User Privacy security and the accuracy of news recommendation.

In summary, differential privacy and federated learning provide strong technical support for Privacy Protection in the news field driven by Artificial Intelligence from different dimensions. With the continuous development and integration of technologies, these technologies will play an increasingly important role in the news industry, promoting the industry to achieve better development while safeguarding privacy.

Technical Application Cases

With the rapid development of artificial intelligence, privacy protection in the news industry has become increasingly critical. Some technical application cases based on relevant research are below:

A news platform utilizing federated learning to protect users' browsing history.

In today's digital era, news platforms accumulate massive amounts of user browsing data, which contains sensitive information such as users' interest preferences [16]. As a privacy-preserving technology, federated learning is gradually being applied in the news domain. A news platform uses federated learning to store browsing history locally, uploading only model gradients for training [16]. As described in the text, multiple users collaboratively train a global model through this approach. During this process, the server cannot access specific user browsing history, thereby protecting user privacy. Additionally, to further enhance recommendation performance, the platform combines news content with user behavioral features and employs deep learning algorithms to model user interests. By continuously optimizing the model, the platform delivers more accurate news recommendations while safeguarding user data security, thus meeting users' needs for accessing preferred news content without compromising data safety.

A news organization applying differential privacy techniques to publish user behavior reports.

News organizations face a dual challenge when analyzing user behavior data—protecting user privacy while providing valuable data insights. To address this issue, one news organization implements differential privacy techniques. The organization adopts an adaptive Gaussian differential privacy-based matrix factorization method when releasing user behavior reports to avoid exposing personal information. During the processing of user behavior data, the organization perturbs the data by adding appropriate noise so that even if the data is leaked, attackers will find it difficult to infer individual user behavior information from the report. For example, when analyzing users' click behaviors on different news categories, the organization utilizes techniques such as adaptive gradient clipping and adaptive noise scale adjustment mentioned in the paper, minimizing the impact of noise on data analysis results while ensuring data usability. In this way, the news agency can publish statistically significant user behavior reports that provide valuable references for industry research and news content optimization, while effectively protecting user privacy [11].

3 Legal and Ethical Standards for Privacy Protection in the News Industry

3.1 Privacy Laws and Regulations

In the current digital era, privacy protection in the news industry is of vital importance, and privacy laws and regulations are key to ensuring their effective implementation. Table 1 presents a comparison of data protection and artificial intelligence regulatory laws in major regions around the world. The detailed explanations are provided in the following text. From an international perspective, the EU's General Data Protection Regulation (GDPR) holds significant influence in the area of privacy protection. GDPR sets strict standards for personal data collection, use, processing, and transmission in the EU/EEA, and is among the toughest privacy laws globally. This regulation comprehensively enhances internet users' data privacy rights, clearly increases corporate data protection responsibilities, and improves the regulatory framework. At the same time, the GDPR expands the scope of data protection, classifying information such as political opinions as sensitive data. These provisions provide a solid legal framework for privacy protection in the news industry, ensuring that news organizations strictly follow relevant norms when handling user data and safeguarding users' privacy [18].

In China, the Personal Information Protection Law plays a crucial role in privacy protection within the news sector. This law stipulates that cross-border transfers of personal information must undergo security reviews conducted by Chinese authorities, and it regulates activities involving the collection, storage, use, processing, transmission, disclosure, and provision of personal information. It also clearly defines the obligations and responsibilities of personal information processors. As processors of personal information, news organizations must strictly comply with this law when conducting news reporting, data collection, and other activities, safeguarding citizens' personal information security and preventing privacy breaches [19].

The California Consumer Privacy Act (CCPA) in the United States also holds significant importance for privacy protection in journalism. The CCPA grants consumers numerous rights regarding their data, such as the right to know what personal data businesses have collected, the right to request deletion of data, and the right to opt out of the sale of their data. This requires news organizations, when handling data of California consumers, to fully respect these consumer rights, strengthen data management and protection, and prevent privacy violations caused by data misuse [20].

In summary, various international privacy protection laws and regulations provide legal basis and standards for privacy protection in journalism from their respective perspectives, prompting news organizations to place greater emphasis on protecting user privacy while pursuing journalistic values, thus safeguarding the public's legitimate rights and interests.

Table 1. Comparison of data protection and AI regulatory regulations in major regions around the world.

Regulation name	Scope of application	Core Clauses (Data Cross-Border / User Rights)		Penalty mechanism
European Union General Data Protection Regulation (GDPR)	All EU member states and non-EU enterprises that process the personal data of EU residents (including news Data Collection, User Profiling).	Cross-border data transfer	It is necessary to comply with the "Adequacy Decision" or Standard Contractual Clauses (SCCs). Transferring data to non-compliant countries is prohibited.	The maximum fine is 4% of the global annual turnover or 20 million euros (e.g., for processing sensitive data without consent or cross-border violations).
		User rights	Data access, deletion (Right to be Forgotten), data portability, and the right to object to automated decision-making (e.g., News Recommendation Algorithm).	
European Union's Artificial Intelligence Act (AI Act)	For AI systems in the EU market, high-risk scenarios (such as news content review and automated news generation) are subject to key supervision.	Cross-border data transfer	It is necessary to meet the requirements of GDPR. High-risk systems need to disclose the logic of Algorithm.	The maximum fine for violations is 30 million euros or 6% of the annual turnover, and high-risk AI systems are prohibited from entering the market.
		User rights	It is prohibited to use AI for social scoring. High-risk systems are required to provide explanations for their decisions.	
The United States California Consumer Privacy Act (CCPA)	Enterprises (including data operations of news media) that process the personal data of California residents and have an annual turnover of over $25 million.	Cross-border data transfer	There is no clear restriction, but the data sharing recipients (such as advertising partners) need to be disclosed.	A fine of $2,500 will be imposed for each violation ($7,500 for intentional violations), and the state attorney general may file a lawsuit.
		User rights	Data access, deletion, and refusal to sell. Enterprises are required to publicize their privacy policies (such as the Data Collection statement on news websites).	
U.S. Gramm-Leach-Bliley Act (GLBA)	US financial institutions (in the news industry, this involves financial data such as subscription payments and advertising placements).	Cross-border data transfer	It is necessary to ensure the security of data in cross-border transmission, referring to the standards of the Federal Reserve.	The maximum civil fine is $1 million. Individual executives may be fined up to $500,000 and imprisoned.
		User rights	Restrict financial institutions from sharing non-public information. Enterprises need to implement data security plans (such as News Platform payment data protection).	
India's Digital Personal Data Protection Act	Enterprises that process personal data of Indian residents (including user data in India of international News Platform).	Cross-border data transfer	Critical personal data must be stored locally, and some data can be transferred to "whitelisted" countries.	A maximum fine of 500 million Indian rupees or 2% of the annual turnover (in case of illegal cross-border data transfer or without explicit consent).
		User rights	Data access, correction, and deletion. Enterprises are required to appoint a Data Protection Officer (DPO).	
European Union Medical Device Regulation (MDR)	AI medical devices in the EU market (such as the health data visualization tool mentioned in the news).	Cross-border data transfer	Cross-border transfer of clinical data must comply with GDPR and pass ethical review.	Revoke the CE certification, ban sales, and impose a fine of up to 4% of the annual turnover.
		User rights	Patients have the right to know the basis of AI diagnosis, and enterprises are required to disclose the Algorithmic Transparency report.	

3.2 Journalism Ethics and Artificial Intelligence

In the field of journalism, privacy protection laws and ethical norms are facing new challenges and opportunities amid the rapid development of artificial intelligence.

From an ethical perspective, the journalistic values of artificial intelligence algorithms should follow the principles of objectivity, fairness, and truthfulness [21]. However, in practical applications, AI algorithms present many potential risks. Among them, algorithmic bias and discrimination stand out prominently [22]. In news production, AI algorithms rely on large datasets for learning and analysis; if training data contains biases, it can easily lead to algorithmic bias. Such bias not only affects public perception of specific groups, but may also further deepen social contradictions.

From a legal and regulatory perspective, although there are currently some laws and regulations regarding data protection and privacy, these provisions still contain many gaps and inadequacies when facing the complex applications of artificial intelligence technology in the news industry. During the processes of news content collection, generation, and dissemination using artificial intelligence, a large amount of user data is involved. Ensuring this data is used reasonably, legally, and in compliance with regulations remains an urgent legal issue today. For example, certain AI-based news recommendation systems may push tailored content based on users' browsing history. In this process, without strict rules governing the collection and use of user data, personal privacy could easily be compromised [23].

To address this, the industry must strengthen self-regulation: journalists should uphold ethics, while news organizations need AI audit mechanisms. When utilizing such technologies to ensure reports adhere to the principles of objectivity, fairness, and accuracy. On the other hand, news organizations should establish and improve internal guidelines for AI application, enhance oversight of AI algorithms, and regularly audit algorithmic mechanisms to prevent algorithmic bias. Meanwhile, governments and relevant regulatory bodies should accelerate improvements in the legal system, clearly defining the legal boundaries for applying artificial intelligence in journalism, and intensifying punishment for illegal activities such as privacy violations and algorithmic discrimination.

In the era of artificial intelligence, the news industry must emphasize the development of legal and ethical frameworks that protect privacy. Only through concerted efforts from all sectors and forming synergies at both legal and ethical levels can the news industry properly safeguard the public's legitimate rights and interests while advancing through the use of artificial intelligence technology.

3.3 Regulatory Challenges

In the field of journalism, privacy protection is critical, and legal and ethical norms related to it face numerous challenges in terms of regulation.

Cross-border data flows have created complex regulatory dilemmas for privacy protection in journalism. As globalization advances and news dissemination becomes increasingly borderless, media organizations often involve cross-border data flows when collecting, storing, and disseminating news content. Differences among data protection laws across countries and regions make it difficult for the journalism industry to ensure data security and privacy during cross-border data transfers [19]. When news organizations process data involving multiple jurisdictions, they must navigate conflicting legal requirements—complying simultaneously with the laws of the data origin location and those of the receiving jurisdiction—which increases compliance complexity. Furthermore, cross-border data flows can lead to ambiguous data jurisdiction. Once a data breach or privacy violation occurs, it becomes difficult to determine which country's legal framework should apply, posing significant challenges for privacy protection regulation in journalism [24].

The requirement for algorithmic transparency also presents a thorny issue in regulating privacy protection within the news industry. Today, artificial intelligence technologies are increasingly applied in journalism, such as in intelligent news recommendation systems and automated content generation. However, many artificial intelligence algorithms lack transparency in their decision-making processes, and their internal mechanisms are difficult to understand. In news recommendation algorithms, the system pushes news content based on user browsing history, search records, and other data, but users often do not know how the algorithm selects and ranks these news items. This opacity may lead to privacy issues. From a regulatory perspective, due to the complexity and technical nature of algorithms, it is difficult for regulators to conduct effective review and oversight, making it challenging to determine whether the algorithm complies with legal and ethical standards for privacy protection. Moreover, when errors occur or privacy is violated, the lack of transparency makes it difficult to identify the responsible party and define the specific scope of liability [21].

4 Analysis of Current Research Status and Comparison

Existing research on privacy protection in the AI-driven news domain has made significant contributions, while also exhibiting certain limitations.

In terms of contributions, firstly, it has enhanced privacy awareness. On one hand, many studies emphasize the importance of user data privacy, pointing out that traditional centralized storage and training of user behavior data in news recommendation pose substantial risks of data leakage, which could expose users' private information such as personal interests, preferences, and browsing habits. This research has deepened the understanding of the importance of protecting user data privacy in the news domain, attracted attention from all parties, and encouraged the industry to explore safer data processing methods [11]. On the other hand, related studies focus on improving users' rights to know and control over data usage, emphasizing that in the AI-driven news domain, users should clearly understand how their data is used, for what purposes, and where it flows, and need to ensure that users can effectively control their data through technical measures and policy regulations, such as granting them the right to choose whether to share data and determine the scope of usage. This has promoted greater transparency and standardization in data usage practices in the news industry, safeguarding users' fundamental rights as data subjects [25].

Secondly, in the application of privacy protection technologies, existing research has achieved valuable results. Federated Learning, as a distributed machine learning technique, plays a key role in protecting privacy in the news domain [26]. It allows multiple data owners to collaboratively train models without exchanging raw data, avoiding privacy risks from centralized data storage. For news data scattered across different media organizations, they can use Federated Learning for local training and only upload model parameters, which are aggregated by a central server to build a global model. This protects each organization's data privacy, enables knowledge sharing, reduces data leakage risks, and allows the news industry to make full use of multi-source data for tasks like news recommendation and trending topic prediction while maintaining user privacy. Differential Privacy is also an important tool for privacy protection in the news industry [26]. By adding random noise to data, it makes it difficult for attackers to infer individual sensitive information from datasets, thus safeguarding data privacy. When analyzing users' browsing data to optimize news recommendation systems, applying Differential Privacy can obscure specific user browsing behaviors without affecting the overall statistical properties of the data, improving recommendation accuracy while preventing privacy leakage. Homomorphic encryption offers a unique solution for privacy protection in the news domain [27]. It allows specific computations on encrypted data, with the decrypted result being the same as if the operations were performed on plaintext. In the news domain, it can be applied to the storage and processing of news data, enabling media organizations to store encrypted data in the cloud and allowing cloud servers to analyze and mine it without knowing the actual content, significantly reducing data leakage risks throughout the processing pipeline.

However, there are also limitations. In terms of adversarial attacks and defense, research on privacy protection in the AI-driven news domain has notable shortcomings. Under the federated learning framework, gradient inversion attacks risk reconstructing users' private information from news data, but current defense strategies are insufficiently adapted to the unstructured nature of news text [26]. Additionally, there are issues such as high computational overheads of encryption techniques, the "privacy-utility" trade-off challenge of differential privacy, and the lack of defenses against cross-platform attacks and dynamic attack evolution, all of which reflect deficiencies in the adaptability and dynamic adversarial capabilities of current defense strategies.

In terms of ethics and legal regulations, existing studies indicate that lagging ethics and legal regulations are a significant issue. Analysis of 57 policy documents from 24 countries shows that ethical and legal frameworks lag in adapting to journalism's specific AI scenarios. For example, emerging issues like excessive personal data collection by automated news gathering technologies and privacy preference misuse due to algorithmic recommendations have not yet formed systematic ethical consensus or legal constraints. Current policies mostly focus on general AI ethical principles but lack detailed privacy risk regulations tailored to the entire process of news content creation and dissemination. Moreover, conflicts over privacy jurisdiction in cross-border journalistic operations highlight insufficient coordination of existing legal frameworks in globalized contexts, potentially placing privacy protection in journalism in a passive state where technological development outpaces regulation, requiring industry-specific improvements to ethical guidelines and legal systems [17].

In terms of explainability and transparency, from a technical implementation perspective, the "black box" nature of algorithms makes it difficult to effectively identify and assess privacy risks. In scenarios like news content recommendation and user behavior analysis, AI models often lack explainability, making it hard for developers and users to trace the end-to-end logic of data collection, processing, and usage, thus preventing accurate identification of potential privacy breach points. Although existing research has proposed theoretical frameworks for explainable AI, practical applications in the news industry still lack customized solutions for privacy protection, and there is a lack of transparency mechanisms at the interaction level between news organizations and users, such as self-service access to privacy impact reports or dynamically updated data usage statements. This dual gap in explainability and transparency not only intensifies user distrust in news platforms' data practices but also hinders regulatory authorities from effectively holding accountable potential privacy-infringing behaviors [28]. Figure 2 highlights the contributions and limitations of the existing research.

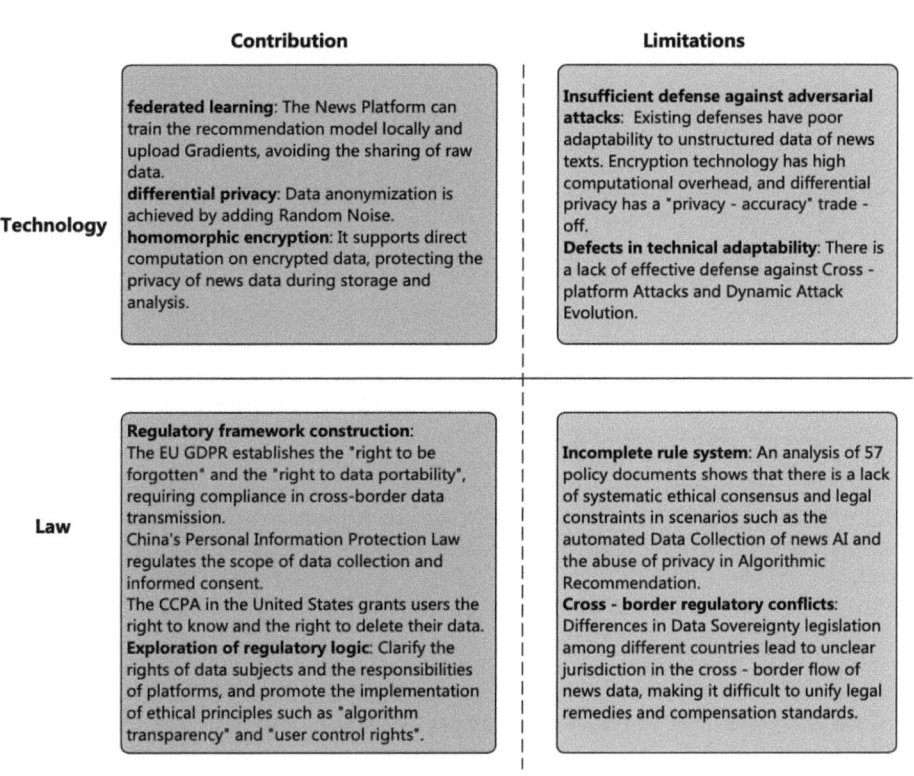

Fig. 2. Two-column comparison chart of contributions and limitations of existing research

5 Future Prospects

With the deep integration of artificial intelligence into journalism, privacy protection is increasingly critical. Future technical research should focus on developing explainable AI frameworks to balance transparency and privacy in news recommendation [29], optimizing federated learning to suit the distributed, diverse, timely, and dynamic nature of news data for efficient collaboration [13], and designing privacy-preserving deep learning models—such as those with modified architectures or privacy protection layers—to resist privacy threats [12]. From a legal perspective, efforts are needed to address cross-border data flows by formulating globalization-adapted rules [19], improve AI-related legal frameworks to cover new privacy issues in news AI applications, clarify stakeholders' responsibilities, and establish scientific data ethics review mechanisms [17, 30]. At the societal ethics level, research should clarify the boundary between journalistic ethics and AI intervention to prevent false information propagation and public opinion manipulation [22], and enhance algorithmic transparency and public oversight through disclosure mechanisms and oversight platforms to ensure fairness in news dissemination [21].

References

1. Song, G.: Application of artificial intelligence in news communication. In: Hung, J.C., Chang, J.W., Pei, Y., Wu, W.C. (eds.) Innovative Computing. Lecture Notes in Electrical Engineering, vol. 791, pp. 197–204. Springer, Singapore (2022)
2. Jain, S.: Artificial intelligence and privacy: an investigation on how artificial intelligence-based data mining is affecting the privacy of users. Int. J. Educ. Soc. Sci. Res. **7**(3), 220–227 (2024)
3. Meng, X., Huo, H., Zhang, X., et al.: A survey of personalized news recommendation. Data Sci. Eng. **8**, 396–416 (2023)
4. Tang, C.: Privacy protection dilemma and improved algorithm construction based on deep learning in the era of artificial intelligence. Secur. Commun. Netw. **2022**, 1–9 (2022)
5. Njiru, D.K., Mugo, D.M., Musyoka, F.M.: Ethical considerations in AI-based user profiling for knowledge management: a critical review. Telemat. Inform. Reports **18**, 100205 (2025)
6. Joshi, N.: Emerging challenges in privacy protection with advancements in artificial intelligence. Int. J. Law Policy **2**(4), 55–77 (2024)
7. Gulati, T.: Artificial intelligence and privacy violation. J. Unique Laws Stud. **2**(2) (2022)
8. Liu, M., Zhang, L.J., Biebricher, C.: Investigating students' cognitive processes in generative ai-assisted digital multimodal composing and traditional writing. Comput. Educ. **211**, 104977 (2024)
9. Yu, R.: Security framework of artificial intelligence system. J. Phys: Conf. Ser. **1927**(1), 012011 (2021)
10. Wu, C., Wu, F., Huang, Y., Xie, X.: Personalized news recommendation: methods and challenges (Version 3). arXiv, https://doi.org/10.48550/ARXIV.2106.08934 (2021)
11. Chen, Y.: A news recommendation method for user privacy protection. Int. J. Comput. Sci. Inform. Technol. **2**(3), 25–36 (2024)
12. Tumma, C., Azmeera, R., Ayyamgari, S., Thumma, B.Y.R.: Data security and privacy protection in artificial intelligence models: challenges and defense mechanisms. Int. J. Sci. Res. Eng. Manage. **9**(1), 1–9 (2025)
13. Habbal, A., Hamouda, H., Alnajim, A.M., Khan, S., Alrifaie, M.F.: Privacy as a lifestyle: empowering assistive technologies for people with disabilities, challenges and future directions. J. King Saud Univ. – Comput. Inform. Sci. **36**(4), 102039 (2024)
14. Liu, H., Wang, Y., Zhang, Z., Deng, J., Chen, C., Zhang, L.Y.: Matrix factorization recommender based on adaptive gaussian differential privacy for implicit feedback. Inf. Process. Manage. **61**(4), 103720 (2024)
15. Ziller, A., Mueller, T.T., Stieger, S., et al.: Reconciling privacy and accuracy in AI for medical imaging. Nat. Mach. Intell. **6**(7), 764–774 (2024)

16. Huang, X., Luo, Y., Liu, L., Zhao, W., Fu, S.: Randomization is all you need: a privacy-preserving federated learning framework for news recommendation. Inf. Sci. **637**, 118943 (2023)
17. Saheb, T., Saheb, T.: Mapping ethical artificial intelligence policy landscape: a mixed method analysis. Sci. Eng. Ethics **30**(2) (2024)
18. Schmidt, J., Schutte, N.M., Buttigieg, S., et al.: Mapping the regulatory landscape for artificial intelligence in health within the european union. NPJ Dig. Med. **7**(1) (2024)
19. Huda, M., Awaludin, A., Siregar, H.K.: Legal challenges in regulating artificial intelligence: a comparative study of privacy and data protection laws. Int. J. Soc. Hum. **1**(2), 116–125 (2024)
20. Chintoh, G.A., Segun-Falade, O.D., Odionu, C.S., Ekeh, A.H.: Challenges and conceptualizing ai-powered privacy risk assessments: legal models for U.S. data protection compliance. Int. J. Frontline Res. Multidiscipl. Stud. **5**(1), 1–9 (2025)
21. Sinha, S., Lee, Y.M.: Challenges with developing and deploying ai models and applications in industrial systems. Discover Artific. Intell. **4**(1) (2024)
22. Ning, D., Fu, Z.: The challenges and responses of artificial intelligence technology to journalism ethics. Artific. Intell. Technol. Res. **2**(3) (2024)
23. Wu, T.: Research on legal and ethical issues of artificial intelligence application in the news field. Mod. Legal Stud. (04) (2024)
24. Balancing Innovation and Privacy: Assessing the legal implications of artificial intelligence in the context of privacy rights and data protection. Int. J. Multidiscipl. Res. **6**(5) (2024)
25. Abolaji, E.O., Akinwande, O.T.: AI powered privacy protection: a survey of current state and future directions. World J. Adv. Res. Rev. **23**(3), 2687–2696 (2024)
26. Rafi, T.H., Noor, F.A., Hussain, T., Chae, D.-K.: Fairness and privacy preserving in federated learning: a survey. Inform. Fus. **105**, 102198 (2024)
27. Yuan, J., Liu, W., Shi, J., Li, Q.: Approximate homomorphic encryption based privacy-preserving machine learning: a survey. Artific. Intell. Rev. **58**(3) (2025)
28. Marasinghe, R., Yigitcanlar, T., Mayere, S., Washington, T., Limb, M.: Towards responsible urban geospatial AI: insights from the white and grey literatures. J. Geovisual. Spatial Anal. **8**(2) (2024)
29. Bozorgpanah, A., Torra, V.: Explainable machine learning models with privacy. Progress Artific. Intell. **13**(1), 31–50 (2024)
30. Ortega-Bolaños, R., Bernal-Salcedo, J., Germán Ortiz, M., et al.: Applying the ethics of AI: a systematic review of tools for developing and assessing AI-based systems. Artific. Intell. Rev. **57**(5) (2024)

Revolutionizing Voting Systems: Integrating Blockchain, RSA-Encrypted NFTs, and Smart Contracts for Enhanced Electoral Integrity

L. K. Bang[1]($^{\boxtimes}$), P. H. T. Trung[1], N. Đ. P. Trong[1], and K. T. N. Ngan[2]

[1] FPT University, Can Tho, Vietnam
bangle69.re@gmail.com
[2] FPT Polytechnic, Can Tho, Vietnam

Abstract. This paper examines the integration of blockchain technology, smart contracts, RSA-encrypted Non-Fungible Tokens (NFTs), and the InterPlanetary File System (IPFS) to address critical challenges in managing voting systems. The approach aims to enhance transparency, ensure the security of voting records, and improve operational efficiency through the adoption of these technologies. Key features of blockchain such as immutability, decentralization, and cryptographic security are leveraged to mitigate risks associated with vote tampering and fraud while enhancing accountability through verifiable transactions. The system's design emphasizes cross-platform compatibility with various Ethereum Virtual Machine (EVM)-supported blockchain platforms, enabling flexibility and scalability. The paper details the system's implementation, evaluates its performance, and discusses the financial implications of its deployment, aiming to present a comprehensive view of how these technologies can improve the integrity and transparency of electoral processes.

Keywords: Blockchain Voting Systems · Electoral Integrity · EVM Platforms · Smart Contracts in Elections · NFTs for Voter Authentication

1 Introduction

Modern democratic societies rely heavily on the reliability and integrity of their voting systems. However, these systems, often grounded in traditional practices, are increasingly confronted with a range of challenges. The principal issues include security vulnerabilities, transparency concerns, and operational inefficiencies [10]. These concerns are not merely theoretical; they have materialized in various incidents that have shaken public confidence in the electoral process. The integrity of elections is essential, as it directly influences the legitimacy of democratic governance [1]. The growing distrust in these systems, driven by technical failures and concerns about vote manipulation, highlights the urgent need for a thorough reevaluation and modernization of the electoral process.

Blockchain technology is increasingly recognized for its potential to enhance electoral systems, offering key features such as immutability, decentralization, and cryptographic security that align well with the needs of a robust voting system [2]. The immutable nature of blockchain means that once a vote is recorded, it cannot be changed, significantly reducing the risks of tampering and fraud. Its decentralized structure increases transparency and accountability [8], allowing multiple parties to verify electoral transactions without compromising voter privacy. This could fundamentally strengthen electoral systems, improving their security and transparency, which are crucial for restoring public trust in democratic processes [15]. However, while recent research has advanced transparency and security in blockchain-based voting systems [3, 6, 9, 11, 13], these studies often concentrate on system design and theoretical frameworks, with less attention given to practical implementation challenges and scalability in real-world scenarios. There remains a need for further exploration into user experience and ease of use, which are essential for broader adoption.

In this paper, we propose a detailed approach to managing transparency in voting systems, focusing on providing a secure and efficient system for managing voting records using blockchain technology, RSA-encrypted NFTs, and smart contracts. Our contributions include the development of a blockchain-centric framework that bolsters the security and integrity of voting records while ensuring they are accessible to authorized individuals. We employ RSA-encrypted NFTs to digitally certify each voting event, making the records secure and transparent. Smart contracts are used to automate and streamline the voting management process, reducing the likelihood of human errors and enhancing operational efficiency. The system is designed for cross-platform compatibility, with implementations across various EVM-supported blockchain platforms, including Binance Smart Chain, Polygon, Fantom, and Celo, ensuring flexibility and scalability [12]. Additionally, by integrating the InterPlanetary File System (IPFS), we provide durable and decentralized storage of voting data, further enhancing accessibility and security.

This study introduces a system that integrates blockchain, smart contracts, Encrypted-RSA NFTs, and IPFS to address common challenges in voting management. The objective is to enhance the transparency of voting records, improve operational efficiency, and ensure the secure handling of voting data. By detailing the system's implementation, rigorously evaluating its performance, and analyzing its fiscal implications, the research highlights the potential benefits these technologies may offer. The findings suggest that such an approach could lead to a voting management system characterized by increased transparency, trust, and accountability.

2 Related Work

Li et al. [9] examine the challenges and solutions related to maintaining transparency while protecting privacy in blockchain-based voting systems. Their study introduces an authority management mechanism within the blockchain framework that aims to keep voter information confidential while ensuring the integrity of the data. This method is vital for maintaining transparency in the voting process without risking the privacy of individual votes. Fusco et al. [3] investigate the use of Shamir's secret sharing method in conjunction with blockchain technology for electronic voting. Their research aims to improve vote privacy and the auditability of the voting process. By integrating secret sharing with blockchain, they propose a method for securing electronic voting that protects the confidentiality of votes and upholds the integrity and transparency of the electoral process.

2.1 Security in Blockchain-Based Voting Systems

Singh et al. [13] examine the use of blockchain technology in digital voting systems, with a focus on improving security features. Their research addresses the necessary architectural and operational elements required to implement a secure blockchain-based voting system. They discuss how blockchain can reduce common security threats in electronic voting, thereby increasing the trustworthiness and integrity of the voting process.

Khan et al. [6] introduce a blockchain-based voting system designed to enhance cryptographic security, with the goal of achieving an end-to-end verifiable voting process. Their study shows how the inherent security features of blockchain can be utilized to create a voting environment that is both transparent and secure. This research is important for illustrating practical ways in which blockchain technology can be applied to increase the security and reliability of digital voting systems.

2.2 Decentralization and Privacy

Patil et al. [11] examine the use of blockchain technology in electronic voting systems, particularly focusing on the advantages of decentralization and anonymity. Their study highlights how blockchain's decentralized structure can support a fair and unbiased electoral process. They point out that blockchain can enhance voter anonymity, thus contributing to the integrity and fairness of elections.

Indapwar et al. [5] explore the development of a decentralized electronic voting system utilizing blockchain technology. Their research points to the substantial difficulty of tampering with data within a blockchain framework, thereby improving the security and integrity of the voting process. This study is valuable in demonstrating how blockchain can be effectively employed to deter electoral fraud and ensure the accuracy of election results.

2.3 Blockchain Applications in E-Voting

Hjalmarsson et al. [4] evaluate the use of blockchain technology in electronic voting systems by analyzing various blockchain frameworks. Their research contributes to the development of a blockchain-based voting system designed to tackle existing electronic voting challenges. They provide a detailed analysis of blockchain solutions that are specifically adapted for electronic voting, indicating a significant contribution to the field.

Kumar et al. [7] concentrate on enhancing the security and integrity of the electronic voting process using blockchain technology. Their strategy involves increasing both transparency and security by maintaining voter details and votes on separate blockchains. This approach preserves voter anonymity while facilitating a transparent and verifiable method for vote tallying, marking an important improvement in the realm of electronic voting systems.

3 Approach

3.1 Traditional Model of Management Vote

The traditional election process is structured around a series of critical interactions and responsibilities that integrate various elements essential for a fair and accurate representation of democratic will. As illustrated in Fig. 1, this model depends on the active participation of informed voters, the functional use of ballots, the secure handling and storage of ballot boxes, thorough counting by officials, and the subsequent disclosure of the results. Each component is designed to work together to maintain the integrity, transparency, and accuracy of the electoral process, thereby ensuring that the collective decision of the electorate is faithfully captured and upheld. The details of these components are explored further in the sections that follow.

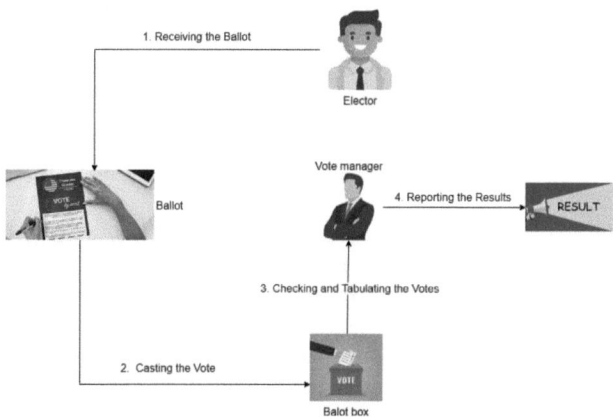

Fig. 1. Traditional model of management vote.

The voting process initiates with Step 1: Receiving the Ballot. Voters arrive at their designated polling stations where they first confirm their eligibility to vote by presenting a voter identification card. This card verifies their registered status and their entitlement to vote. Once their eligibility is confirmed, voters receive their ballots. At this point, the significance of their civic responsibility becomes particularly evident. Voters are afforded time to reflect on their choices, recognizing that each selection on their ballot represents not only a preference for a candidate or policy but also an expression of their hopes and concerns for their community and nation. This initial step is crucial as it establishes a foundation for a fair and transparent voting process.

In Step 2, voters' considerations turn into definitive choices. Within the privacy of the voting booth, they mark their ballots. This step respects the principle of a secret ballot, a fundamental aspect of democratic elections, which ensures that voters can make their choices freely, without external pressure or influence. The act of marking the ballot, while private, has significant public implications. Once completed, voters place their ballots into a secure ballot box, symbolizing their active participation in the democratic process and contributing to the collective voice of their society.

Step 3 begins after the voting period ends. Election officials carefully examine each ballot to ensure that each vote adheres to the rules and is free from any discrepancies. This scrutiny is essential for maintaining the legitimacy of the election. The integrity of the election depends heavily on the precision and impartiality of this process. Ballots may be counted manually or electronically, based on the resources and protocols of the electoral authority. This phase aggregates the individual choices of the voters, forming the collective will of the electorate.

The final step amalgamates the diligent efforts from the previous stages into a conclusive outcome. Election officials compile the data from the tabulated votes to determine the election winners or the prevailing opinions on various issues. The announcement of the results is more than a disclosure of figures; it marks the culmination of the democratic process. These results set the future direction for policies, leadership, and governance, as directly determined by the electorate. The transparency and accuracy of this announcement are critical to maintaining the electorate's trust in the democratic process and ensuring that the elected representatives or policies accurately reflect the will of the people.

3.2 Phase One: Blockchain-Based Approach for Management Voting Integrating Smart Contract, RSA-Encrypted NFT, IPFS, and Blockchain Techniques

The traditional election model, though well-established, faces several issues that could compromise its efficiency and reliability. Challenges such as potential fraudulent activities, human errors during vote counting, delays in results tabulation, and concerns about voter privacy and ballot security are common. Furthermore, dependence on physical infrastructure and manual processes often results in inefficiencies and elevated costs. In addressing these problems, a blockchain-based approach to election management is being considered. This method incorporates Smart Contract, RSA-encrypted Non-Fungible Tokens, InterPlanetary File System (IPFS), and Blockchain technologies to enhance the electoral process. Blockchain technology helps improve the integrity and transparency of the voting system by providing a secure, unalterable, and clear ledger for votes. Smart Contracts automate several elements of the voting process, minimizing the possibility of human error and fraud. RSA-encrypted NFTs can represent unique voter identities, ensuring one vote per person while preserving anonymity. Additionally, IPFS presents a decentralized storage solution that improves data security and accessibility, addressing some of the critical vulnerabilities of traditional voting systems.

Building on the model discussed in our previous article [14], we aim to enhance the transparency in election management by integrating RSA-encrypted NFTs. Our approach employs technologies such as Smart Contracts, RSA-encrypted Non-Fungible Tokens (NFTs), the InterPlanetary File System (IPFS), and Blockchain to address the limitations of traditional voting systems. Figure 2 illustrates the architecture of this approach, featuring several components designed to improve the electoral process. These components include a User Interface for straightforward navigation and data entry, a Personal Identification Code for secure voter identification, Smart Contracts to automate and validate electoral procedures, RSA-encrypted NFTs for digitizing and verifying individual votes, IPFS for decentralized and resilient data storage, and a Distributed Ledger to maintain a transparent and immutable record of all transactions and interactions. This setup aims to enhance the accuracy and integrity of voting processes, ensuring that each step from voter registration to result announcement is verifiable and secure.

- **Personal Identification Code** In blockchain-based voting systems, the Personal Identification Code plays a key role in authenticating voter identity and verifying eligibility, helping to prevent unauthorized access and fraudulent activities to uphold the integrity and fairness of the election.
- **Electronic Voting Card** The Electronic Voting Card, a digital component of blockchain voting, stores voter and candidate information. Integrated into the blockchain and protected by smart contracts and RSA-encrypted Non-Fungible Tokens, it provides secure and immutable management of voter information.
- **User Interface** The User Interface in blockchain elections is designed for simplicity, enabling voters to easily cast their votes and access election information. It also offers real-time updates and a transparent view of the ongoing electoral process.
- **Vote Manager** Within a blockchain voting system, the Vote Manager is responsible for compiling and reporting election results, ensuring that the results are accurate and transparently aggregated, blending technological skills with a deep understanding of electoral practices.
- **Smart Contracts for Transparency in Decision-Making** Smart contracts play a vital role in automating essential electoral processes such as vote counting and voter eligibility checks, thereby enhancing transparency and minimizing the risk of errors or manipulation.
- **RSA-encrypted NFTs** RSA-encrypted Non-Fungible Tokens are employed to record each vote as a unique, secure, and unchangeable record, thus adding a robust layer of security and distinctiveness to the voting process.

- **IPFS** The InterPlanetary File System aids in the decentralized and efficient dissemination of election results, ensuring their availability and resistance to censorship, which improves the accessibility and reliability of the information distributed.
- **Distributed Ledger** The distributed ledger offers a synchronized and decentralized database ideal for preserving the integrity of election-related data, ensuring all data such as votes, voter registrations, and results are consistently recorded and accessible across various network nodes.

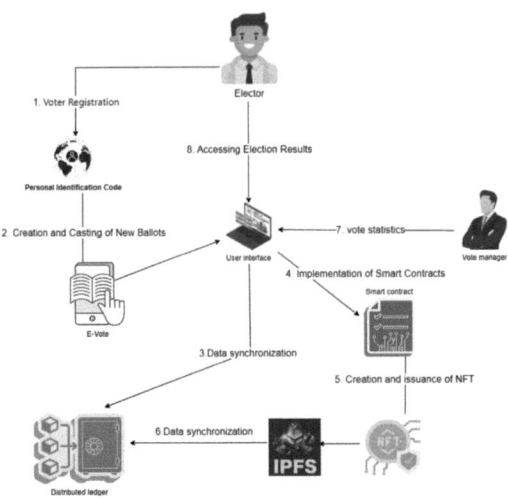

Fig. 2. Blockchain-based model for management voting: Integrating Smart Contract, NFT, IPFS, and Blockchain Techniques.

The newly developed blockchain-based model for elections introduces a significant alteration in the voting mechanism by incorporating technologies such as distributed ledgers, smart contracts, and RSA-encrypted Non-Fungible Tokens (NFTs). This approach provides improvements in the security, transparency, and efficiency of the electoral process compared to traditional methods. The immutable nature of the blockchain ledger guarantees that each vote is securely recorded and protected against tampering. Smart contracts facilitate the automation and optimization of the voting process, thereby reducing the risks associated with human errors and fraudulent activities. The utilization of RSA-encrypted NFTs for voter identification, along with the InterPlanetary File System (IPFS) for data storage, further enhances the system's security and integrity. This updated method not only improves the accessibility and convenience of the voting process for electors but also strengthens public confidence in the electoral system, representing a notable advancement in the practices of democratic voting (refer to Fig. 2 for more details).

Step 1: Voter Registration In the initial phase, voters register in the system with their unique personal identification codes. This code is crucial for ensuring the privacy and security of personal information while verifying voter eligibility. The registration process is structured to create a secure and authenticated voter base, essential for a reliable electoral process. This step prevents fraudulent voting and double registrations by verifying each voter's identity and securely recording it in the system.

Step 2: Creation and Casting of New Ballots After registration, voters use the system's interface to create their ballots. This process can be done remotely, improving the accessibility of voting and allowing a wider range of voters to participate, including those unable to reach polling stations. The interface is designed to be intuitive, enabling voters to make their choices clearly and confidently.

Step 3: Synchronization of Data to the Distributed Ledger Once ballots are created, the details of the voters and their ballots are synchronized to a distributed ledger. This ledger acts as an immutable record that maintains the transparency and integrity of the voting data, crucial for upholding the trustworthiness of the electoral process.

Step 4: Implementation of Smart Contracts Smart contracts are applied to automate various tasks within the electoral process, such as verifying voting rights, confirming ballot validity, and securely recording votes. This automation helps streamline the election, making it more efficient and resistant to tampering or fraud.

Step 5: RSA Encrypted NFT Creation and Storage on IPFS Validated ballots are converted into RSA-encrypted Non-Fungible Tokens and stored on the InterPlanetary File System (IPFS). This step secures the uniqueness and security of each vote, ensuring each is preserved as a distinct and unalterable record.

Step 6: Re-Synchronization to the Distributed Ledger After the RSA-encrypted NFTs are created, details of these tokens are re-synchronized to the distributed ledger, ensuring all election-related data remain consistent and transparent, maintaining a complete and unalterable record from start to finish.

Step 7: Statistical Analysis and Evaluation of Election Results Election administrators use the system interface to perform statistical analysis and evaluation of the election results, automated through smart contracts to enhance result accuracy and minimize human error. This step is essential for providing a clear and precise interpretation of the electoral outcome.

Step 8: Accessing Election Results Finally, voters and other stakeholders can access and review the election results through the system's interface. This accessibility increases transparency and trust in the electoral process by allowing easy verification of the outcomes, ensuring the results are readily available and understandable to all interested parties, reinforcing the credibility of the election.

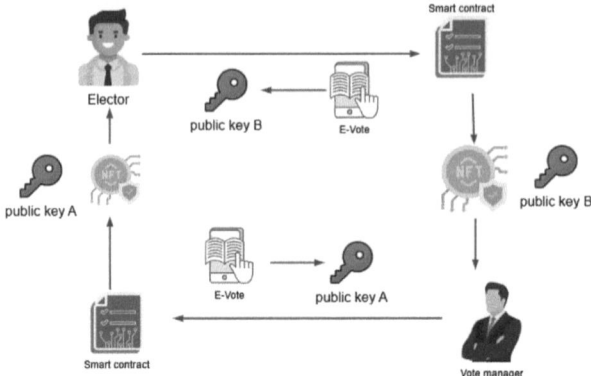

Fig. 3. Schematic representation of a Voting Management model using RSA-encrypted NFTs.

3.3 Phase Two: Integration of RSA-Encrypted NFTs and Smart Contracts for Voting Management

The diagram (Fig. 3) illustrates a methodical approach to managing voting records using RSA-encrypted Non-Fungible Tokens (NFTs) to ensure secure and private access. In this system, voters and election centers are the primary users who interact with the voting records through distinct public keys within the blockchain framework.

Initially, each voter is assigned a unique public key (referred to as public key A in the diagram), which is essential for accessing their personal voting records. The NFTs, which represent the individual votes, are encrypted using RSA encryption, a widely recognized method for securing sensitive data. The encrypted NFT is linked to the voter's public key, ensuring that only they can access and manage their voting data, thereby maintaining the confidentiality and integrity of each vote.

In a similar setup for voting systems, election centers are allocated a separate public key (referred to as public key B). When an election official needs to access voter records, the NFT is decrypted using the corresponding private key that matches public key B. This decryption process allows for secure and controlled access to voting records by authorized personnel. RSA encryption ensures that the data is transmitted and viewed without the risk of unauthorized access or exposure.

Smart contracts within the blockchain manage the permissions and actions associated with these NFTs. They execute predefined rules that determine who can access the voting records, under what conditions, and what actions can be taken. For example, a smart contract may be programmed to grant access to an election official when a voter needs to verify their voting history or to update voting records when new votes are cast.

The architecture ensures that all interactions with the voting records are logged and traceable. The use of blockchain technology provides an immutable ledger of transactions, adding a layer of accountability and traceability to the record-keeping process. This method mitigates the risk of record tampering and provides a clear audit trail for all activities related to voter data.

This model represents a structured mechanism to enhance transparency in election management. By using RSA-encrypted NFTs, it addresses critical concerns around data security and privacy in the voting process. The clear delineation of access rights via public and private keys, managed by smart contracts, provides a secure framework for managing voter records. This approach aims to improve the integrity and confidentiality of voting data, creating a more transparent and secure environment for election management.

4 Evaluation

4.1 Evaluation of RSA-Encrypted NFT Framework for Efficiency in Vaccine Management in Children

In the context of applying RSA-encrypted NFTs to vaccine management in children, a thorough performance review was conducted. This assessment focused on two types of data reflective of vaccination documentation needs: an image file, representing visual documentation such as vaccination certificates, and a text record, analogous to standard vaccination details and schedules. The analysis aimed to measure how effectively these digital assets, when secured with RSA encryption and embedded in NFTs, could be managed and utilized to ensure security and transparency in the vaccination process from administration to record-keeping.

The efficiency of RSA key generation, encryption, and decryption processes for image files used in the voting management system is summarized in Table 1. The time required for RSA key generation varied considerably, ranging from 30,108 microseconds to 301,008 microseconds, with an average of about 146,687 microseconds, highlighting the substantial computational effort needed for this foundational step. Encryption of the image files proved quicker, with times ranging from 8,111 microseconds to 11,635 microseconds, and an average duration of approximately 9,744 microseconds, supporting the necessity for efficient handling of voting documents. However, the decryption process was notably more time-consuming, with durations ranging from 255,306 microseconds to 269,676 microseconds, averaging 262,883 microseconds. This extended decryption time emphasizes the computational intensity of the RSA algorithm, reflecting a balance between the need for robust data security and the efficiency of processing in voting systems.

The evaluation of time efficiency in the RSA key generation, encryption, and decryption processes for text within the voting management system is summarized in Table 2. The time required for generating the RSA key varied from 24,110 microseconds to 168,443 microseconds, with an average of approximately 78,356 microseconds, illustrating the substantial computational demand of this initial step. The encryption of text data was consistently rapid across all trials, indicating a negligible time requirement for this process. Decryption times ranged

Table 1. "Evaluation of Time Efficiency in RSA Key Generation, Encryption, and Decryption for Image in Microseconds

RSA (image)	1	2	3	4	5	6	7	8	9	10
Generating key	75356	95235	38750	78216	98703	95067	54002	301008	75905	98625
Encrypting image	10678	9685	8111	9330	9393	10638	11635	10350	10979	10646
Decrypting image	262878	265051	269676	255449	258359	265588	255306	258615	259331	260586

from 501 microseconds to 1,508 microseconds, with an average of 1,011 microseconds, demonstrating the system's efficiency in handling routine data entries while ensuring secure and swift access to voting records. This setup highlights the balance between maintaining robust data security and facilitating quick data processing within the electoral management framework.

Table 2. "Evaluation of Time Efficiency in RSA Key Generation, Encryption, and Decryption for Text in Microseconds

RSA (text)	1	2	3	4	5	6	7	8	9	10
Generating key	109072	161201	58533	54586	24110	94431	168443	31826	46018	82341
Encrypting text	0	0	0	0	0	0	0	0	0	0
Decrypting text	594	1413	1160	1274	501	1084	1378	1508	502	998

Upon reviewing the performance metrics, it is evident that the RSA encryption mechanism maintains a relatively consistent level of efficiency regardless of the data type being secured. However, the generation of keys and the decryption phases require significant computational resources, an aspect inherent to RSA's design aimed at ensuring high levels of security. The extended duration of the decryption process particularly highlights the computational effort needed to access secure data within RSA-encrypted frameworks. This balance between security and processing speed is critical in the practical application of RSA encryption within voting management systems, where both data protection and operational efficiency are essential. The results presented in Tables 1 and 2 reflect these factors, emphasizing the necessity for robust yet efficient encryption methods to manage voting records effectively.

4.2 Testing on EVM-Supported Platforms

In our pursuit of establishing a secure and efficient system for managing transparency in voting, our paper conducts a detailed analysis of blockchain technology as a core component. Specifically, we explore the integration of Blockchain, RSA-encrypted NFTs, and IPFS to enhance traceability and ensure the authenticity of voting records. Within this framework, we focus on three crucial functions: data creation, NFT minting, and NFT transfer. These functions are essential for recording and verifying voting data, certifying its integrity, and facilitating the secure exchange of information across the electoral system.

To conduct our analysis, we examine four Ethereum Virtual Machine (EVM)-compatible blockchain platforms: BNB Chain (formerly known as Binance Smart Chain), Fantom, Celo, and Polygon. Each platform offers unique features and benefits that are well-suited to support the outlined functions, albeit with varying degrees of efficiency and cost implications, as evidenced by the transaction fees associated with each process.

- BNB Chain is known for its high throughput and low transaction costs, making it an attractive option for applications requiring scalability and efficiency. It is designed to provide a robust platform for decentralized applications (dApps) and NFT transactions.
- Fantom prioritizes security, scalability, and decentralization. With its bespoke consensus mechanism, it offers near-instant transaction finality, which is crucial for operations in electoral systems where timely and reliable updates are essential for maintaining the integrity of voting data.
- Celo, with its mobile-first approach, aims to increase blockchain adoption among smartphone users. This characteristic is particularly relevant to voting management in remote areas, where access to traditional computing devices may be limited. Celo's focus on accessibility and low transaction fees supports the objective of creating an inclusive and efficient voting management system.
- Polygon, known for its multi-chain scalability solutions, provides a framework that facilitates fast and efficient transactions. It is particularly adept at handling complex operations, such as those involved in minting and transferring NFTs, at a fraction of the cost and time.

Our paper aims to present a comprehensive analysis of the suitability and effectiveness of these blockchain platforms in fostering a secure and efficient system for managing voting transparency. By examining the transaction fees associated with data creation, NFT minting, and NFT transfer, we seek to offer insights into the economic feasibility of implementing these technologies. Our analysis is grounded in a realistic assessment of the platforms' capabilities, providing a clear view of the potential and challenges of integrating blockchain technology into voting management.

Transaction Fee Analysis: Table 3 compares transaction fees on Binance Smart Chain (BNB), Fantom (FTM), Polygon (MATIC), and Celo (CELO) for a framework enhancing vaccine management in children using RSA-encrypted NFTs and smart contracts. These platforms are chosen for their compatibility with the Ethereum Virtual Machine (EVM), which is crucial for our smart contracts. The table also shows the token market values for these platforms as of May 27, 2024, at 7:00:00 AM UTC, highlighting the economic context for adopting these blockchain technologies in the vaccine management system.

Table 3. Transaction fee

	Transaction Creation	Create NFT	Transfer NFT
BNB	0.0273134 BNB ($16.47)	0.00109162 BNB ($0.66)	0.00057003 BNB ($0.34)
Fantom	0.00957754 FTM ($0.00)	0.000405167 FTM ($0.00)	0.0002380105 FTM ($0.00)
Polygon	0.006840710032835408 MATIC ($0.01)	0.000289405001852192 MATIC ($0.00)	0.000170007501088048 MATIC ($0.00)
Celo	0.007097844 CELO ($0.005)	0.0002840812 CELO ($0.000)	0.0001554878 CELO ($0.000)

Firstly, on Binance Smart Chain, transaction fees are 0.0273134 BNB ($16.47), minting an NFT costs 0.00109162 BNB ($0.66), and transferring an NFT costs 0.00057003 BNB ($0.34). These fees position Binance Smart Chain as an efficient platform, albeit potentially costlier than alternatives. Secondly, Fantom presents a cost-effective alternative, with the price for executing a new transaction set at 0.00957754 FTM, a nominal amount in dollar terms. Fees for NFT creation and transfer on Fantom's network are recorded at 0.000405167 FTM and 0.0002380105 FTM, respectively, both translating to minimal dollar values. This suggests that Fantom offers a more affordable solution for managing transactions, particularly for activities involving NFTs. Thirdly, the Polygon network lists the fee for starting a transaction at 0.006840710032835408 MATIC, or just $0.01. Creating an NFT on Polygon is extremely cost-effective at 0.000289405001852192 MATIC, and transferring an NFT costs 0.000170007501088048 MATIC. Both expenses are negligible, indicating a minimal financial impact for operations on this platform. Finally, Celo's network charges 0.007097844 CELO for initiating a transaction, which equates to about $0.005. The fees for NFT creation and transfer are 0.0002840812 CELO and 0.0001554878 CELO, respectively, both amounting to less than a cent. These figures position Celo as an economically viable choice for transaction management within the system.

5 Conclusion

The research detailed in this paper highlights the potential of blockchain technology, smart contracts, RSA-encrypted NFTs, and IPFS to significantly enhance the management of voting systems. By deploying a blockchain-centric framework, the study demonstrates how these technologies can be used to address prevailing issues such as security vulnerabilities, transparency concerns, and operational inefficiencies in traditional voting systems. The findings reveal that the proposed system not only secures voting records and ensures their integrity but also facilitates a more transparent and accountable electoral process. Although challenges related to scalability and user experience are acknowledged, the initial results indicate a promising direction for further development. Future work will focus on refining the technology for practical application, enhancing user interface design, and expanding real-world trials to fully realize the benefits of blockchain in electoral systems.

References

1. Elklit, J., Reynolds, A.: The impact of election administration on the legitimacy of emerging democracies: a new comparative politics research agenda. Commonw. Comp. Polit. **40**(2), 86–119 (2002)
2. Ferreira, L., Cruz, M.R., Cruz, E.F., Quintela, H., Cunha, M.C.: Supporting Technologies and the Impact of Blockchain on Organizations and Society. IGI Global (2023)
3. Fusco, F., Lunesu, M.I., Pani, F.E., Pinna, A.: Crypto-voting, a blockchain based e-voting system. In: KMIS, pp. 221–225 (2018)
4. Hjálmarsson, F., Hreiarsson, G.K., Hamdaqa, M., Hjálmtỳsson, G.: Blockchain-based e-voting system. In: 2018 IEEE 11th International Conference on Cloud Computing (CLOUD), pp. 983–986. IEEE (2018)
5. Indapwar, A., Chandak, M., Jain, A.: E-voting system using blockchain technology. Int. J. Adv. Trends Comput. Sci. Eng. **9**(3) (2020)
6. Khan, K.M., Arshad, J., Khan, M.M.: Secure digital voting system based on blockchain technology. Int. J. Electron. Gov. Res. (IJEGR) **14**(1), 53–62 (2018)
7. Kumar, D.D., Chandini, D., Reddy, D., Bhattacharyya, D., Kim, T.: Secure electronic voting system using blockchain technology. Int. J. Smart Home **14**(2), 31–38 (2020)
8. Le, N.T.T., et al.: Assuring non-fraudulent transactions in cash on delivery by introducing double smart contracts. Int. J. Adv. Comput. Sci. Appl. **10**(5), 677–684 (2019)
9. Li, C., Xiao, J., Dai, X., Jin, H.: Amvchain: authority management mechanism on blockchain-based voting systems. Peer-to-peer Network. Appl. **14**, 2801–2812 (2021)
10. Moynihan, D.P.: Building secure elections: e-voting, security, and systems theory. Public Adm. Rev. **64**(5), 515–528 (2004)
11. Patil, H.V., Rathi, K.G., Tribhuwan, M.V.: A study on decentralized e-voting system using blockchain technology. Int. Res. J. Eng. Technol. **5**(11), 48–53 (2018)
12. Quoc, K.L., et al.: SSSB: an approach to insurance for cross-border exchange by using smart contracts. In: Mobile Web and Intelligent Information Systems: 18th International Conference, pp. 179–192. Springer (2022)
13. Singh, A., Chatterjee, K.: Secevs: secure electronic voting system using blockchain technology. In: 2018 International Conference on Computing, Power and Communication Technologies (GUCON), pp. 863–867. IEEE (2018)
14. Trong, N., et al.: Blockchain-enhanced pediatric vaccine management: a novel approach integrating NFTs, IPFs, and smart contracts. In: International Conference on Services Computing, pp. 63–78. Springer (2023)
15. Weir, K.: Safeguarding democracy: increasing election integrity through enhanced voter verification. Homeland Security Affairs (2018)

Revolutionizing Knowledge Management: Utilizing Encrypted NFTs, Smart Contract and IPFS Within Blockchain Technologies

L. K. Bang[1]($\boxtimes$), P. H. T. Trung[1], N. Đ. P. Trong[1], and K. T. N. Ngan[2]

[1] FPT University, Can Tho, Vietnam
bangle69.re@gmail.com
[2] FPT Polytechnic, Can Tho, Vietnam

Abstract. This paper examines the potential of integrating blockchain technology, encrypted Non-Fungible Tokens (NFTs), and the InterPlanetary File System (IPFS) to advance knowledge management systems, particularly within academic settings. We propose an architecture that addresses the limitations of traditional knowledge management systems by enhancing data security, copyright protection, and accessibility. The system leverages blockchain's immutable and transparent properties, IPFS's decentralized storage capabilities, and the unique identification features of NFTs secured with six encryption algorithms—RSA, RC4, DES, ChaCha20, Blowfish, and AES. The study involves deploying smart contracts on four Ethereum Virtual Machine (EVM)-compatible platforms—Binance Smart Chain, Polygon, Fantom, and Celo—to assess each platform's effectiveness in managing encrypted NFTs and to identify the optimal encryption method for operational efficiency. Our findings aim to demonstrate how these technologies can potentially enhance the robustness and efficiency of knowledge management in academic environments.

Keywords: Knowledge management · Knowledge · Blockchain · Smart contracts · NFT · IPFS · BNB Smart Chain · Celo · Fantom · Polygon

1 Introduction

The integration of blockchain technology with knowledge management is reshaping how academic content is stored, accessed, and shared. The use of digital technologies such as Non-Fungible Tokens (NFTs) and the InterPlanetary File System (IPFS) prompts a rethinking of traditional knowledge management systems. Our study investigates how these technologies could improve the efficiency and security of managing knowledge, especially within academic environments. Traditional academic knowledge management has typically depended on both physical and digital repositories overseen by librarians, serving as a foundational element of scholarly communication. This established model, marked by its systematic interactions between human agents and information repositories, has supported an ongoing exchange of learning and contributions among scholars [12,13]. Yet, as digital technologies evolve, the conventional system begins to show its constraints, notably in areas such as accessibility, copyright protection, and the maintenance of data integrity.

Recent research into blockchain technology in knowledge management suggests it could improve traditional systems. Studies such as those by Pfeiffer et al. [13] and Nyame et al. [12] point to blockchain's capabilities for enhancing secure and transparent knowledge transfer and access control. Additionally, work by Bartling & Fecher [3] and Qin et al. [14] demonstrate its broader applications in knowledge creation and organizational management, establishing a foundation for blockchain's role in fostering a more decentralized and secure approach to knowledge management. Concurrently, cloud computing's integration into knowledge management systems is being recognized for its adaptability to technological changes, as discussed by Depeige & Boulanger [4] and Khoshnevis & Khanlari [5]. Their research highlights the scalability and flexibility of cloud services in managing knowledge, although issues with data security and system integrity remain significant challenges, emphasizing the need for more robust solutions [1,7].

In this paper, we propose an architectural framework that integrates blockchain technology, encrypted Non-Fungible Tokens (NFTs), and the InterPlanetary File System (IPFS) into a knowledge management system to address the limitations of traditional models, particularly in terms of data security, copyright protection, and accessibility. Our approach utilizes the immutable and transparent properties of blockchain, the decentralized storage capabilities of IPFS, and the unique identification offered by NFTs, which are secured using six different encryption algorithms-RSA, RC4, DES, ChaCha20, Blowfish, and AES. This system is designed to assess which encryption method best balances security with operational efficiency, thereby enhancing the management and dissemination of knowledge in a way that maintains integrity and accessibility [9].

To assess the feasibility of our system, we have implemented smart contracts on four Ethereum Virtual Machine (EVM)-compatible platforms: Binance Smart Chain, Polygon, Fantom, and Celo. Each platform provides a distinct testing environment for various functionalities of our system, including transaction creation and the management of Non-Fungible Tokens (NFTs), which are encrypted using six different algorithms-RSA, RC4, DES, ChaCha20, Blowfish, and AES. This evaluation focuses on analyzing the system's performance, scalability, and cost-efficiency in practical scenarios [12,13]. Additionally, we have utilized the Pinata platform to deploy academic and intellectual property data on the InterPlanetary File System (IPFS), testing the system's interoperability and the effectiveness of decentralized storage in improving the accessibility and reliability of knowledge assets [4,5]. This comprehensive approach helps determine the most suitable encryption method for balancing security with operational efficiency within our knowledge management framework.

In this paper, we explore a blockchain-based architecture that utilizes smart contracts and encrypted Non-Fungible Tokens (NFTs) to improve the management of academic content. We implement these smart contracts on four Ethereum Virtual Machine (EVM)-compatible platforms-Binance Smart Chain, Polygon, Fantom, and Celo-to evaluate system functionality and performance in various blockchain environments. Each NFT is secured with one of six encryption algorithms-RSA, RC4, DES, ChaCha20, Blowfish, and AES-to determine which offers an optimal mix of security and efficiency. Our findings suggest that this approach not only addresses limitations of traditional knowledge management systems but also leverages decentralized technologies like IPFS to enhance data accessibility, reliability, and security, while protecting copyright effectively.

2 Related Work

2.1 Blockchain and Knowledge Management

In the context of blockchain applications in knowledge management, Pfeiffer et al. [13] explore a blockchain-based reward system to encourage knowledge transfer across generations through methods like gamification and nudging, securely recording rewards. Nyame et al. [12] focus on enhancing security within knowledge management systems by using blockchain to support robust role-based access control and ensure the immutability of knowledge resources. Bartling & Fecher [3] discuss how blockchain could address the reproducibility crisis in science, aiming for a more transparent research evaluation process. Qin et al. [14] propose a blockchain framework for automating knowledge in organizational management, integrating smart contracts to support a cyber-physical-social system. Additionally, Suciu et al. [15] present a model that uses private blockchains for managing the evolution and transfer of organizational knowledge, considering its socio-economic and cultural impacts. Azeem et al. [2] have developed'Jigsaw', a decentralized system on blockchain for knowledge sharing that rewards contributors and maintains the longevity of knowledge assets. Finally, Mittal et al. [9] address knowledge provenance issues in the misinformation era, using blockchain to secure knowledge origins and enhance credibility and traceability, with potential extensions across various domains. These studies collectively underline the potential of blockchain in enhancing the security, management, and dissemination of knowledge.

2.2 Cloud Computing and Knowledge Management

The intersection of Cloud Computing and Knowledge Management has been explored in various studies [10,11,16], highlighting significant developments in this area. Depeige & Boulanger [4] introduced the concept of Actionable Knowledge As A Service (AKAAS), which utilizes big data analytics within cloud environments to enhance decision-making frameworks and technical applications, pointing to the need for knowledge management processes to evolve with technological advancements. Khoshnevis & Khanlari [5] proposed an architecture for Knowledge Management as a Service (KMaaS) that integrates cloud computing to bolster business and competitive intelligence, an approach not fully capitalized on in current practices. Aksoy & Öztürk [1] discuss both the benefits and risks, such as security issues, associated with adopting cloud computing in knowledge management. Liu et al. [7] assess the partial implementation of a cloud-based system in education, presenting evidence of its benefits on learning quality. Tsui [17] advocates for utilizing cloud ecosystems for personal knowledge management, which surpass traditional methods in capability. Miklovsik et al. [8] suggest a cloud-based approach to improve the management and creation of knowledge with intelligent tools, while Li [6] highlights how cloud computing can enhance personal knowledge management through scalable services and social support mechanisms.

2.3 Comparative Analysis of Our Approach to Existing Studies

Our architectural approach to knowledge management, which incorporates blockchain technology, encrypted Non-Fungible Tokens (NFTs), and the Inter-Planetary File System (IPFS), both contrasts with and complements existing research in the realms of blockchain and cloud computing for knowledge management. While studies by Pfeiffer et al. [13], Nyame et al. [12], and others have investigated how blockchain can enhance security, transparency, and incentivization in knowledge transfer, our framework advances these concepts by developing a comprehensive system for the storage, retrieval, and dissemination of knowledge. This system not only promotes knowledge sharing but also ensures the protection of intellectual property rights and maintains the integrity of knowledge assets through the immutable nature of blockchain. Unlike traditional cloud-based systems, our method utilizes the decentralized attributes of blockchain and IPFS to address risks related to centralized storage systems, such as single points of failure and data breaches. Additionally, our use of NFTs provides a method for managing digital rights that expands on the capabilities of existing cloud-based approaches.

3 Approach

3.1 Foundations and Functions: The Classical Architecture of Academic Knowledge Management

In academic settings, knowledge management has traditionally focused on meticulous cataloging and distribution of scholarly works, utilizing both physical books and digital documents. Librarians are crucial in upholding the integrity of these processes, facilitating the structured access and preservation of information. This established system enables a consistent cycle where scholars learn and contribute, supporting effective scholarly discourse over time. This paper examines the key elements and interactions within the traditional knowledge management structure, highlighting how they support ongoing academic engagement.

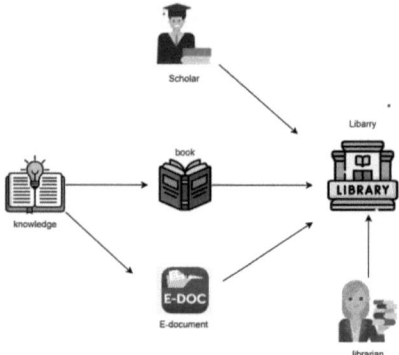

Fig. 1. Schematic Representation of Traditional Knowledge Management Systems: Interactions between Scholars, Resources, and Librarians.

The diagram Fig. 1 illustrates a traditional knowledge management system characterized by structured interactions between human agents and information repositories, centered around the concept of knowledge. This knowledge is primarily stored in books and electronic documents, with books being managed within libraries that curate and provide access to these resources, and electronic documents offering a digital method for storing and accessing scholarly data. The diagram shows a dynamic relationship between books and libraries, as well as a blended approach to managing both digital and physical resources. Librarians play a key role in organizing, classifying, and enabling access to these resources, ensuring the system supports academic research efficiently. Scholars, at the top of this system, rely on these resources and contribute new insights, fostering a continuous exchange of information and dialogue within the academic community.

The traditional architecture for knowledge management in academic and research institutions, while established, does not fully address the needs of modern systems that incorporate digital and decentralized technologies. This model primarily relies on physical resources such as books, which limits access to certain locations and impedes global sharing. While the adoption of electronic documents has begun to ease these access issues, their integration into existing systems is often incomplete and fails to effectively merge digital and physical resources. Additionally, the traditional approach to copyright protection is proving inadequate, as the replication of both physical and digital works poses significant challenges in protecting intellectual property rights, often leaving creators exposed to unauthorized use. Existing copyright mechanisms are not keeping up with technological advancements that improve access to knowledge, resulting in a defensive stance on protecting creators' rights. Therefore, the traditional model, despite its structured framework for sharing academic resources, exhibits substantial inefficiencies, highlighting the need for a more adaptable approach in today's digital context.

3.2 Architecture of a Blockchain-Enhanced Knowledge Management System

The examination of the current knowledge management landscape reveals that integrating certain digital technologies could enhance the established systems for storing, retrieving, and disseminating information. The architectural approach outlined Fig. 2 suggests incorporating blockchain technology, encrypted NFTs, and IPFS to improve the management of scholarly content. This proposed framework aims to preserve the integrity and accessibility of academic materials while addressing copyright protection challenges. By utilizing the capabilities of distributed ledgers and digital identifiers, the system is designed to create a more secure and efficient environment for scholars to access and contribute knowledge.

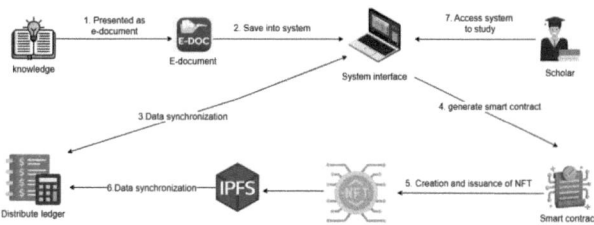

Fig. 2. Integrated Knowledge Management System Architecture Combining Blockchain, NFTs, and IPFS.

The architecture detailed here proposes a structured approach to knowledge management through the integration of blockchain technology with encrypted Non-Fungible Tokens (encrypted NFTs) and the InterPlanetary File System (IPFS). The process begins with an e-document, which is stored in a system that leverages the immutable and transparent properties of blockchain technology. This incorporation establishes a secure and traceable foundation, where each addition or transaction within the knowledge base is recorded in a manner that is resistant to tampering and is easily verifiable.

Following this, data synchronization across all nodes of the distributed ledger ensures the consistency and accuracy of the stored knowledge. This decentralized process reduces the risks associated with single-point failures and maintains the robustness of the system against potential data loss or corruption. The inherent redundancy in distributed ledgers facilitates the replication of knowledge across multiple nodes, enhancing the preservation of data.

The next step involves the generation of a smart contract, which is essential in this framework. These contracts establish the rules governing the access, usage, and distribution of the e-document and automate their enforcement, thus eliminating the need for intermediaries. This automation helps reduce delays and mitigates disputes over knowledge usage.

In the following phase, an encrypted NFT is created and associated with the e-document. This encrypted NFT acts as a unique identifier for the e-document, ensuring clear ownership and origin, while also integrating usage rights and other relevant metadata. The role of encrypted NFTs extends beyond mere proof of ownership to include the enforcement of the smart contracts linked to the document.

IPFS is integral to this architecture by providing a distributed network for storing the e-document. It enables decentralized storage, which protects the document from outages and censorship. Furthermore, IPFS enhances data retrieval efficiency through its content-addressable data structure, ensuring that the e-document is resilient and easily accessible.

The culmination of this architecture is reflected in the system interface, which facilitates scholar interaction with the e-document. Through this interface, the theoretical benefits of blockchain, encrypted NFTs, and IPFS are transformed into practical applications, allowing users to interact with and utilize knowledge in a secure and regulated environment.

Compared to the traditional model, the integrated approach utilizing blockchain and IPFS offers distinct advantages. The decentralized nature of these technologies means that knowledge is distributed across a network rather than being housed in a single repository, which enhances both accessibility and reliability. The use of smart contracts and encrypted Non-Fungible Tokens (encrypted NFTs) adds a layer of security and rights management that is automated and transparent, addressing some of the copyright protection challenges found in conventional systems. Furthermore, the immutability of blockchain ensures that once information is added, its origin and ownership records are permanent, providing a clear audit trail. This contrasts with traditional systems where the origins of knowledge can be unclear, and managing rights is often a complex, manual task. Overall, this architecture offers a more streamlined and secure method for managing knowledge, focusing on user needs.

4 Implementation

In the implementation section of our paper, we focus on the application of various encryption algorithms for securing metadata within Non-Fungible Tokens (encrypted NFTs), crucial for a blockchain-based knowledge management system. We assess six encryption methods-RSA, RC4, DES, ChaCha20, Blowfish, and AES-to identify a balance between security and efficiency. This evaluation is key to maintaining the system's performance and reliability as we manage scholarly data. We specifically measure each algorithm's encryption speed and security level, concentrating on their effectiveness in protecting encrypted NFTs and data stored on the InterPlanetary File System (IPFS). The findings, including performance metrics for encrypting both text and image data essential to the integrity and transparency of the academic records, are detailed in comprehensive tables (Table 1).

In our evaluation of encryption algorithms for securing academic records within a blockchain-based knowledge management system, we analyzed RSA, an asymmetric encryption method. Our findings showed that RSA's key generation times varied considerably, ranging from 75,356 microseconds to as much

Table 1. RSA Encryption and Decryption Performance for Image and text Data in Microseconds

RSA	1	2	3	4	5	6	7	8	9	10
Generating key	75356	95235	38750	78216	98703	95067	54002	301008	75905	98625
Encrypting image	10678	9685	8111	9330	9393	10638	11635	10350	10979	10646
Decrypting image	262878	265051	269676	255449	258359	265588	255306	258615	259331	260586
Generating key	109072	161201	58533	54586	24110	94431	168443	31826	46018	82341
Encrypting text	0	0	0	0	1367	0	0	0	0	998
Decrypting text	594	1413	1160	1274	501	1084	1378	1508	502	0

as 301,008 microseconds. Furthermore, the encryption and decryption processes for image data were notably slow, with decryption times frequently exceeding 250,000 microseconds. These results indicate that while RSA offers robust security, its slower processing speeds could challenge the computational efficiency of our system, potentially impacting the performance of managing encrypted Non-Fungible Tokens (NFTs) and data on the InterPlanetary File System (IPFS) (Table 2).

Table 2. RC4 Encryption and Decryption Performance for Image and text Data in Microseconds

RC4 (image)	1	2	3	4	5	6	7	8	9	10
Encrypting image	107	0	0	0	171	0	543	0	0	0
Decrypting image	0	0	664	0	0	0	0	0	1502	0
Encrypting text	0	0	0	0	0	0	0	0	0	0
Decrypting text	0	0	0	0	0	0	0	0	0	0

In our analysis of encryption methods for enhancing the security of a knowledge management system, we observed that the RC4 algorithm provided notably low encryption and decryption times for both image and text data, often approaching near zero microseconds. This efficiency suggests that RC4 could improve transaction processing speeds within our system. However, the security offered by RC4 is not on par with that of more modern encryption algorithms, which raises concerns about its suitability. The discrepancy between RC4's rapid processing and its lesser security level may restrict its use, especially when considering the crucial need to maintain the integrity and security of data. This is a concern similar to that identified with RSA, where the algorithm's slower speeds potentially affect overall system performance (Table 3).

In our study of encryption algorithms for a knowledge management system, we found that DES offers moderate processing times, with encryption of image data ranging from 540 to 1,217μs and decryption times up to 1,058 microseconds. These figures indicate that DES could potentially enhance the operational efficiency of our system due to its relatively quick processing. However, DES

Table 3. DES Encryption and Decryption Performance for Image and text Data in Microseconds

DES (image)	1	2	3	4	5	6	7	8	9	10
Encrypting image	1073	540	820	1047	1091	708	1217	599	1121	1024
Decrypting image	1058	551	0	819	606	999	1005	1018	501	0
Encrypting text	0	0	0	0	0	0	0	0	0	0
Decrypting text	0	0	0	0	0	508	0	0	0	0

is known to have security vulnerabilities that pose a substantial risk to data integrity. These security concerns may negate the benefits of its faster processing times, a dilemma similar to the trade-offs seen with RC4's speed versus security issues and the slow performance of RSA impacting the system's overall efficiency (Table 4).

Table 4. Chacha20 Encryption and Decryption Performance for Image and text Data in Microseconds

CHACHA20 (image)	1	2	3	4	5	6	7	8	9	10
Encrypting image	501	0	109	0	0	0	0	0	0	101
Decrypting image	0	584	511	0	0	668	0	634	0	0
Encrypting text	0	0	0	0	0	0	0	0	0	0
Decrypting text	0	0	0	0	0	508	0	0	0	0

In our analysis of encryption methods for a knowledge management system, ChaCha20 demonstrated a promising balance of speed and security. It required only 501 microseconds to encrypt image data, with decryption times showing some variability but remaining efficient. These results position ChaCha20 as a feasible option for securing metadata within systems managing scholarly content, due to its rapid processing and strong security features. This makes it a practical alternative compared to the challenges associated with other algorithms like the security vulnerabilities of DES, the inadequate security of RC4, and the slow processing speeds of RSA, especially when the focus is on maintaining the integrity and confidentiality of sensitive information (Table 5).

Table 5. Blowfish Encryption and Decryption Performance for Image and text Data in Microseconds

blowfish (image)	1	2	3	4	5	6	7	8	9	10
Encrypting image	542	603	506	599	507	1145	608	1137	633	541
Decrypting image	0	0	508	512	501	501	1037	999	575	532
Encrypting text	0	0	537	520	0	533	91	0	0	0
Decrypting text	0	0	0	0	0	0	0	0	0	0

In our evaluation of encryption algorithms for a knowledge management system, Blowfish demonstrated moderate performance, with encryption times for image data varying from 506 to 1,145 microseconds. Blowfish has historically been recognized for providing a reasonable balance of speed and security. Nonetheless, with the development of newer encryption algorithms that offer improved security features, its suitability for modern systems may be questioned. This raises concerns about Blowfish's capability to effectively secure sensitive academic information in the face of increasing cybersecurity threats, a challenge that echoes the vulnerabilities seen with DES and the trade-offs between speed and security noted in RC4, RSA, and ChaCha20 (Table 6).

Table 6. AES Encryption and Decryption Performance for Image and text Data in Microseconds

AES (image)	1	2	3	4	5	6	7	8	9	10
Encrypting image	0	360	0		82	592	608	502	541	510	513
Decrypting image	1332	0		1005	0	504	0	0	0	0	0
Encrypting text	0	0	0	0	0	0	0	507	0	0
Decrypting text	0	0	0	0	0	0	0	0	0	0

In our evaluation of encryption algorithms for a knowledge management system, AES stood out for its performance and reliability, achieving near-instantaneous encryption and decryption times as low as 504 microseconds. Known for its strong security features, AES offers efficient processing suitable for protecting sensitive academic data. This efficiency is essential for our system, which demands both secure information storage and quick data access. This finding contrasts with other algorithms like Blowfish, ChaCha20, and DES, which, while also focusing on data integrity, do not match AES in balancing security needs with operational speed amid increasing cybersecurity threats.

Our study evaluates the efficiency of various encryption algorithms within a blockchain-based knowledge management system, analyzing RSA, RC4, DES, ChaCha20, Blowfish, and AES. These methods are tested in the context of managing academic data, which requires a flexible encryption strategy to handle frequent and varied transactions. The goal is to find an encryption method that not only meets high security standards but also supports efficient operational performance. This research is essential for developing a reliable and transparent system that can be utilized effectively by academic institutions and researchers.

5 Evaluation

In our study, we aim to deploy smart contracts on four EVM-compatible platforms: Binance Smart Chain, Polygon, Fantom, and Celo, to assess their suitability for knowledge management. Each platform's features and capabilities will be examined to determine how they support our system requirements. Additionally, we plan to use the InterPlanetary File System (IPFS) for decentralized data storage, specifically for academic and intellectual property data, utilizing the Pinata platform to improve access to this network. This approach will help us understand the potential of these platforms in managing and storing sensitive data securely.

5.1 Environment Simulation

Fig. 3. Configuration of Nodes within a Simulated Blockchain Environment for NFT and IPFS Integration.

The simulated environment depicted is designed to test the interoperability of encrypted Non-Fungible Tokens (encrypted NFTs) and the InterPlanetary File System (IPFS) within a blockchain network. Each node in this network is equipped with a unique public-private key pair, which is essential for maintaining security. These nodes represent various entities in a knowledge management system, engaged in tasks like issuing encrypted NFTs and interacting with smart contracts. To facilitate thorough testing without the limitation of resource scarcity, the simulation allocates a substantial amount of ether to each node. The primary goal of this setup is to evaluate the operational effectiveness of encrypted NFTs and IPFS in managing data within a blockchain framework, simulating conditions close to real-world applications. This testing is crucial for confirming the system's design and functionality, ensuring readiness for practical deployment.

5.2 Implementing IPFS for Knowledge Management Systems

The code excerpt in Fig. 4 details the metadata protocol for an e-document tailored for use in a blockchain and IPFS-based management system. The 'body' section records key document details such as type, title, author, content, and

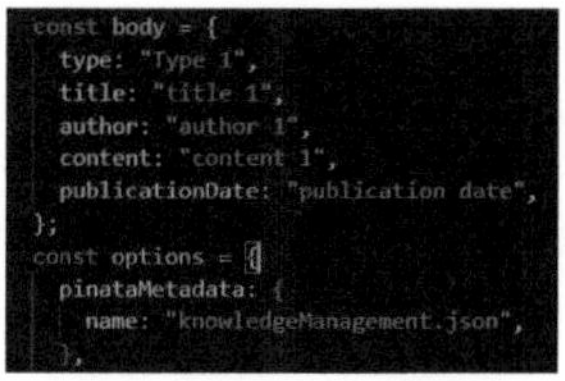

Fig. 4. E-Document Metadata Framework for Blockchain and IPFS Integration.

Fig. 5. Knowledge record (ID) hash link generation on IPFS platform.

publication date, facilitating easy identification and retrieval within the decentralized network. Additionally, the 'options' section contains 'pinataMetadata', setting up the document for storage on IPFS under the label "knowledgeManagement.json," which helps in maintaining a traceable presence on the platform. Linked to an encrypted Non-Fungible Token (encrypted NFT) within the blockchain, this metadata verifies the document's authenticity and ownership, and each interaction with the document is recorded on the blockchain to ensure its integrity and manage digital scholarly resources effectively.

The image illustrates an e-document being successfully submitted to the IPFS network, with the generation of a unique Content Identifier (CID) as depicted in Fig. 5. This CID, a product of the IPFS protocol, confirms that the document has been securely stored in the network. It serves as a hash representation of the e-document, ensuring accurate retrieval of the file as initially uploaded. The process duration, marked as "3936," highlights the network's efficiency in handling transactions, which is vital for managing time-sensitive knowledge assets. In this setup, the CID is key to the decentralized management of e-documents, providing a secure method for managing digital content within the blockchain environment.

Fig. 6. Knowledge record (ID) hash link generation on IPFS platform.

Fig. 7. Retrieved E-Document Metadata Displayed via IPFS Gateway.

The image shows the Pinata platform's dashboard, as highlighted in Fig. 6, which developers use for managing digital assets on the InterPlanetary File System (IPFS). The dashboard displays the file 'knowledgeManagement.json', anchored in the network with visible details like file size and retention period, demonstrating its role in decentralized content management. Pinata simplifies the use of IPFS with a user-friendly interface that facilitates easy access to e-documents via content identifiers, ensuring they are persistent and retrievable within the distributed web space.

The image illustrates a web browser window showing a JSON layout of an e-document's metadata, as retrieved through an IPFS gateway facilitated by Pinata, detailed in Fig. 7. Displayed in the browser are the key-value pairs that outline the document's type, title, author, content, and publication date. This layout verifies that the document's metadata has been successfully retrieved from the decentralized storage, illustrating the straightforward nature of data retrieval via IPFS. The URL shown confirms that the data is accessed through a custom Pinata subdomain, which aids in streamlining the process of fetching data from the IPFS network.

5.3 Testing on EVM-Supported Platforms

Our research explores the Ethereum Virtual Machine (EVM) as a platform for deploying smart contracts, focusing on four EVM-compatible platforms: Binance Smart Chain, Polygon, Fantom, and Celo. We examine the process of creating data or transactions to assess how these platforms manage new entries such as academic articles or intellectual property records. Key evaluation criteria include transaction speed, computational resources, and user-friendliness. Additionally, we analyze each platform's ability to create and manage encrypted Non-Fungible Tokens (NFTs), vital for document authentication and rights management. The study also assesses the transferability of these NFTs to facilitate operations like changing document ownership or access rights, evaluating the security, ease of transfer, and overall user experience.

Our study evaluates the suitability of four EVM-compatible platforms-Binance Smart Chain, Polygon, Fantom, and Celo-for a knowledge management system aimed at managing scholarly data and ensuring efficient blockchain operations. We recorded token prices as of March 27, 2024, providing an economic perspective. A proof-of-concept has been developed and deployed on each platform's testnet to verify our theoretical model's practicality. This includes BNB, MATIC, FTM, and CELO, ensuring that each platform can support the processes required for effective knowledge management. Additionally, we present a comparison of transaction fees for essential operations like recording knowledge assets, creating encrypted Non-Fungible Tokens (NFTs), and transferring these tokens, which are crucial for digitizing and licensing intellectual property (Table 7).

Transaction Fee. Starting with Binance Smart Chain, the analysis shows a moderate fee structure, with contract creation identified as the costliest operation at 0.0273134 BNB or approximately \$8.27. This factor might influence decisions in scenarios where a high volume of transactions is expected. However, the fees for NFT generation and transfers are comparatively lower, costing \$0.33 and \$0.17 respectively, which suggests a more budget-friendly option for the digital representation and transfer of knowledge assets.

Fantom's fee structure is notably minimal, with the creation and transfer of NFTs incurring virtually no cost in USD terms. This extremely low cost could be

Table 7. Transaction fee

	Transaction Creation	Create NFT	Transfer NFT
BNB Smart Chain	0.0273134 BNB ($8.27)	0.00109162 BNB ($0.33)	0.00057003 BNB ($0.17)
Fantom	0.00957754 FTM ($0.00)	0.000405167 FTM ($0.00)	0.0002380105 FTM ($0.00)
Polygon	0.006840710032835408 MATIC ($0.01)	0.000289405001852192 MATIC ($0.00)	0.000170007501088048 MATIC ($0.00)
Celo	0.007097844 CELO ($0.005)	0.0002840812 CELO ($0.000)	0.0001554878 CELO ($0.000)

beneficial for a knowledge management system that demands frequent transactions. It should be noted that the absence of any explicit USD cost might result from rounding off very low figures, implying that while the costs are minimal, they are not entirely absent.

Polygon's platform is highlighted by its minimal fees, with only $0.01 charged for contract creation and negligible fees for NFT creation and transfer. This cost structure makes Polygon an appealing option for knowledge management systems that require low-cost operations without sacrificing the advantages of blockchain technology, such as security and transaction verifiability.

Celo, while slightly more expensive than Fantom and Polygon, still maintains a low fee structure in USD terms, supporting the financial feasibility for managing knowledge assets. The minimal costs associated with NFT creation and transfer on Celo suggest that it could be a cost-effective platform for the dissemination and collaborative exchange of knowledge.

In conclusion, our economic analysis reveals important details for organizations considering blockchain for knowledge management systems. Binance Smart Chain may be more suitable for less frequent but higher value transactions due to its cost structure. In contrast, Fantom, Polygon, and Celo, with their low to negligible fees, are better suited for systems that require many transactions, as they can minimize operational costs. These insights guide the selection of platforms based on the frequency of transactions and cost considerations.

6 Conclusion

Our study on the integration of blockchain, encrypted NFTs, and IPFS in academic knowledge management reveals that this system enhances security, integrity, and accessibility of academic content compared to traditional frameworks. By implementing smart contracts on various EVM-compatible platforms, we evaluated the system's practicality and identified an effective encryption algorithm that balances security with efficiency. Each platform displayed unique strengths, providing insights into the operational benefits of using advanced technologies in knowledge management systems. The use of decentralized technologies shows potential for addressing current challenges like data security and accessibility in academic settings. Future research will aim to further refine these technological integrations and extend their application to other areas of knowledge management.

References

1. Aksoy, et al.: Knowledge management in the cloud: benefits and risks. Int. J. Comput. Appl. Technol. Res. **3**(11), 718–720 (2014)
2. Azeem, et al.: Blockchain based decentralized knowledge sharing system-jigsaw. In: 2019 4th International Conference on Information Technology Research (ICITR), pp. 1–6. IEEE (2019)
3. Bartling, S.: Blockchain for science and knowledge creation. In: Gesundheit digital: Perspektiven zur Digitalisierung im Gesundheitswesen, pp. 159–180. Springer (2018)
4. Depeige, et al.: Actionable knowledge as a service (AKAAS): leveraging big data analytics in cloud computing environments. J. Big Data **2**(1), 1–16 (2015)
5. Khoshnevis, et al.: Toward knowledge management as a service in cloud-based environments. Int. J. Mechatron. Electr. Comput. Technol. **2**(4), 88–110 (2012)
6. Li, et al.: Cloud computing support for personal knowledge management. In: 2009 International Conference on Information Management, Innovation Management and Industrial Engineering, vol. 4, pp. 171–174. IEEE (2009)
7. Liu, et al.: Effectiveness of the partial implementation of a cloud-based knowledge management system. Int. J. Emerg. Technol. Learn. (iJET) **15**(13), 155–171 (2020)
8. Miklošík, et al.: Knowledge base cloud–a new approach to knowledge management systems architecture. Acta Universitatis Agriculturae et Silviculturae Mendelianae Brunensis **60**, 28 (2012)
9. Mittal, et al.: Managing knowledge provenance using blockchain. In: 2018 9th IEEE International Conference on Cognitive Infocommunications (CogInfoCom), pp. 000241–000246. IEEE (2018)
10. Nguyen, L.T.T., et al.: BMDD: a novel approach for IoT platform (broker-less and microservice architecture, decentralized identity, and dynamic transmission messages). PeerJ Comput. Sci. **8**, e950 (2022)
11. Nguyen, T.T.L., et al.: Toward a unique IoT network via single sign-on protocol and message queue. In: Computer Information Systems and Industrial Management: 20th International Conference, pp. 270–284. Springer (2021)
12. Nyame, et al.: An ECDSA approach to access control in knowledge management systems using blockchain. Information **11**(2), 111 (2020)
13. Pfeiffer, et al.: The use of blockchain-supported reward systems for knowledge transfer between generations. Academic Conferences International Limited (2020)
14. Qin, et al.: Blockchain-based knowledge automation for CPSS-oriented parallel management. IEEE Trans. Comput. Soc. Syst. **7**(5), 1180–1188 (2020)
15. Suciu, et al.: Knowledge decentralization in the age of blockchain: developing a knowledge-transfer system using digital assets. Knowledge, People, and Digital Transformation: Approaches for a Sustainable Future, pp. 261–274 (2020)
16. Thanh, L.N.T., et al.: Toward a security IoT platform with high rate transmission and low energy consumption. In: Gervasi, O., et al. (eds.) ICCSA 2021. LNCS, vol. 12949, pp. 647–662. Springer, Cham (2021). https://doi.org/10.1007/978-3-030-86653-2_47
17. Tsui, et al.: Cloud-based personal knowledge management as a service (PKMAAS). In: 2011 International Conference on Computer Science and Service System (CSSS), pp. 2152–2155. IEEE (2011)

Blockchain Solutions: Encrypted NFTs and Smart Contracts for Safer Pet Health Records

L. K. Bang[1(✉)], P. H. T. Trung[1], N. Đ. P. Trong[1], and K. T. N. Ngan[2]

[1] FPT University, Can Tho City, Vietnam
bangle69.re@gmail.com
[2] FPT Polytechnic, Can Tho City, Vietnam

Abstract. This paper presents a framework that integrates blockchain technology, smart contracts, encrypted Non-Fungible Tokens (NFTs), and the InterPlanetary File System (IPFS) to address the challenges of managing child health records. By leveraging the decentralized, immutable, and transparent properties of blockchain, alongside a suite of encryption algorithms-RSA, RC4, DES, ChaCha20, Blowfish, and AES-our system enhances the security and efficiency of record management. The use of smart contracts facilitates automated and error-free transactions, while encrypted NFTs ensure the uniqueness and privacy of each health record. The system's performance was tested across several EVM-compatible blockchain platforms including Binance Smart Chain, Polygon, Fantom, and Celo, focusing on key functionalities such as data recording, secure record-keeping, and NFT transferability. The analysis not only demonstrates improved security and efficiency but also underscores the potential for reducing operational costs associated with managing child health records.

Keywords: Pet Healthcare · Blockchain · Data Management · (EHRs) · NFTs · IPFS · Decentralized Storage · Smart Contracts

1 Introduction

In veterinary care, the protection of pet health records is a critical issue, with both traditional and electronic systems facing significant challenges related to security, privacy, and accessibility. Our research proposes using blockchain technology, encrypted Non-Fungible Tokens (NFTs), and smart contracts as a method to improve the security and management of pet health records. This initiative stems from the need to overcome the limitations of current systems. Traditional management practices, which often involve manual documentation and physical storage, can lead to inefficiencies, potential data loss, and privacy breaches [16]. Meanwhile, Electronic Health Records (EHRs) enhance accessibility and centralize data but still encounter problems with data security and vulnerability to unauthorized access [5]. These issues highlight the necessity for a more secure and dependable approach to managing pet health records.

The use of electronic health records (EHRs) in veterinary science presents challenges related to data management, access control, and data quality. Romar [18] and Menendez [15] have addressed these issues, focusing on access controls for animal health records and the quality of data in dairy farm records. Syndromic surveillance has been adapted for veterinary use to detect outbreaks early, with Kass [11] and Anholt [4] discussing its application in companion animals. The global importance of EHRs is further supported by Kim [12], who studied medical conditions in dogs in Korea, and Gray [9], who explored euthanasia decision-making in the UK. These studies underline the essential role of EHRs in advancing animal care.

Our proposed framework utilizes the decentralized nature of blockchain technology, which offers a more secure alternative to traditional and electronic pet health record systems. The blockchain provides inherent security features such as immutability and transparency, which are critical for handling sensitive health data [14]. In this system, RSA encryption, along with other algorithms like RC4, DES, ChaCha20, Blowfish, and AES, is integrated with Non-Fungible Tokens (NFTs) to secure the health records, ensuring that access is restricted to authorized users only. This setup not only safeguards privacy but also maintains the uniqueness and integrity of each pet's health record. Additionally, smart contracts automate the creation, access, and transfer of these records [6,7]. These contracts, which execute terms directly encoded in their programming, facilitate secure and efficient interactions within the healthcare system, minimize the potential for errors, and provide a reliable mechanism for managing access to pet health information.

Our proposed system's flexibility and performance were thoroughly evaluated on four EVM-compatible blockchain platforms: Binance Smart Chain, Polygon, Fantom, and Celo. This evaluation was aimed at understanding how well the system could adapt to and utilize the unique features of each platform to improve the management of pet health records. We focused on key functions such as recording health data, creating NFTs encrypted with a range of algorithms (RSA, RC4, DES, ChaCha20, Blowfish, and AES) for secure record-keeping, and the transferability of these NFTs. These tests provided insights into the system's operational speed, resource efficiency, and reliability. Additionally, we analyzed the transaction costs associated with these platforms, which highlighted the potential for cost reductions and increased operational efficiency in managing pet health records.

In conclusion, our study introduces a method that utilizes blockchain technology, smart contracts, encrypted Non-Fungible Tokens (NFTs), and the InterPlanetary File System (IPFS) to enhance the management of child health records. This approach effectively tackles challenges associated with data security, accessibility, and integrity, thereby establishing a new benchmark for how child health records can be managed securely and efficiently. Through the application of various encryption algorithms-RSA, RC4, DES, ChaCha20, Blowfish, and AES-our research evaluates their appropriateness in terms of security and operational efficiency. We have thoroughly investigated the integration of these technologies and highlighted their potential in creating a child health record management system that is secure and practical for stakeholders in the healthcare sector.

2 Related Work

2.1 Technological Advancements in Veterinary Health Records

The application of electronic health records (EHRs) in veterinary practice has been instrumental in enhancing the understanding of animal health and disease trends. For instance, Quintana et al. developed a natural language processing pipeline using EHR data to monitor animal bites, a critical component of rabies surveillance and prevention [17]. In a related study, Hanauer et al. analyzed the correlation between cat bites and human depression through EHR data, uncovering noteworthy associations and gender-related differences [10]. Menendez et al. assessed the data quality within animal health records on dairy farms [15], and Aigner developed a prototype EHR system for managing livestock health [1]. Additionally, Krone explored the adoption of electronic veterinary medical records in Massachusetts, identifying challenges and benefits associated with their use [13]. These studies collectively highlight the critical role EHRs play across various ve

2.2 Advancements and Challenges of EHRs in Pediatric Care

Anholt et al. [3] demonstrated the capability of EHRs in identifying spatial-temporal clusters of enteric syndrome in companion animals, highlighting their value in providing early warnings of environmental hazards. Furthermore, Anholt et al. [2] applied a text-mining approach to effectively analyze veterinary records for enteric syndrome surveillance, showcasing the practicality of EHRs in disease monitoring. Kass et al. [11] developed a syndromic surveillance system capable of detecting epidemics among companion animals, including foodborne outbreaks. Complementing these studies, Anholt's thesis [4] delivered an extensive examination of the use of informatics and EHRs in syndromic surveillance, outlining both the challenges and capabilities of these systems in enhancing public health monitoring.

2.3 Data Analysis and Utilization in Veterinary Practices

In a similar vein, Gray et al. [9] analyzed veterinary consultations through EHRs to explore the complexities involved in making euthanasia decisions for dogs and cats, emphasizing the role of palliative care in giving pet owners time to make informed choices. Kim et al. [12] investigated health data by breed and life stage in dogs in Korea, highlighting the need for tailored healthcare strategies to improve early disease detection and management. Gates et al. [8] used EHR data from routine vaccination visits to estimate obesity prevalence in adult dogs and cats in New Zealand, underscoring the importance of consistent body condition and weight recording for monitoring and preventing obesity. Lastly, Salt et al. [19] applied bi-clustering analysis to veterinary EHRs to stratify companion animal life stages based on disease diagnosis data, which informed healthcare recommendations while accentuating the relevance of age and breed in disease susceptibility.

3 Approach

3.1 Traditional Process for Managing Pet Health Records

The traditional system remains in use, but it largely depends on manual processes that are prone to a range of inefficiencies and potential errors. These processes often involve the physical handling and movement of paper records between different parties, such as healthcare providers, administrative staff, and other stakeholders. This method of record-keeping can create several issues, including delays in the transfer of information, which may slow down decision-making and patient care. There is also a significant risk of important documents being lost or misplaced during these transfers, further complicating the process. Additionally, relying on paper-based records raises significant concerns about the security and privacy of sensitive health information. Paper records are susceptible to unauthorized access, damage, or loss, making them less secure compared to digital alternatives. This situation suggests a pressing need for systems that can better manage these records in a secure and efficient manner, ensuring that health data is handled in a way that both protects patient privacy and facilitates the accurate and timely exchange of information between all involved parties. In doing so, healthcare providers could improve their operational efficiency while minimizing the risks associated with the current paper-based system (Fig. 1).

3.2 Building a Secure Framework for Pet Health Records Using Blockchain and Encryption with NFTs

The diagram 1 outlines a structured approach for managing pet health records through blockchain technology, starting with the pet owner who identifies a health issue with their pet and seeks veterinary assistance. In this model, both pets and their owners are assigned a unique global identifier, which is crucial for integrating and accessing the pet's health information across multiple platforms.

At the veterinary clinic, nurses are responsible for the initial step in this digital system by creating digital medical records. These records are linked to the pet's unique global identifier, setting the stage for all subsequent medical interactions. Should the pet require diagnostic tests, the veterinarian uses the system to send a digital request directly to a laboratory. The lab conducts the tests and uploads the results to the pet's digital medical record, ensuring that all data remains connected to the global identifier.

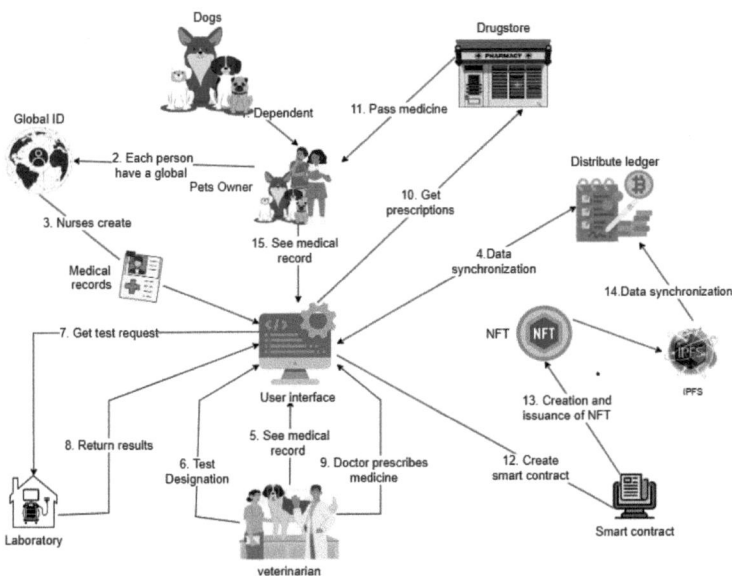

Fig. 1. Diagram of a Blockchain-Integrated Model for Pet Health Record Management

The system incorporates a user interface that interacts with the blockchain's distributed ledger. This feature allows various stakeholders, such as pet owners and veterinarians, to securely access and update medical records. The security of these records is further strengthened by the creation of encrypted Non-Fungible Tokens (NFTs). These encrypted NFTs, representing the unique medical records, are generated through smart contracts that automatically execute the terms embedded within their code.

When medications are prescribed by the veterinarian, these prescriptions are also stored on the blockchain. Pet owners can then procure the prescribed medication from a pharmacy, with each transaction being recorded and verified within the blockchain. This step ensures that every action within the pet's health journey is traceable and permanently recorded, thereby maintaining a secure and comprehensive medical history.

Finally, the system ensures that data is synchronized not only across the blockchain's distributed ledger but also through the InterPlanetary File System (IPFS), enhancing the security and decentralization of the records. This eliminates potential data silos and points of failure, ensuring that the records are robust and widely accessible. Pet owners have the ability to access and review their pet's medical records at any time through the user interface, keeping them informed and actively involved in the management of their pet's health.

4 Implementation

In our implementation section, we explore the application of various encryption algorithms to secure metadata for Non-Fungible Tokens (NFTs), which are integral to our blockchain-based system for managing pet health records. We specifically assess six encryption methods-RSA, RC4, DES, ChaCha20, Blowfish, and AES-to determine the most effective balance between security and operational efficiency. This analysis is crucial as it directly influences the system's performance and reliability. The effectiveness of each algorithm is measured based on its encryption speed and security level, focusing on how well they secure encrypted NFTs and data on the InterPlanetary File System (IPFS). Our findings are presented in detailed tables, showcasing the performance metrics of these algorithms when encrypting both text and image data, which are critical for maintaining the integrity and transparency of pet health records (Table 1).

Table 1. RSA Performance for Image and text Data in Microseconds

RSA	1	2	3	4	5	6	7	8	9	10
Generating key	75356	95235	38750	78216	98703	95067	54002	301008	75905	98625
Encrypting image	10678	9685	8111	9330	9393	10638	11635	10350	10979	10646
Decrypting image	262878	265051	269676	255449	258359	265588	255306	258615	259331	260586
Generating key	109072	161201	58533	54586	24110	94431	168443	31826	46018	82341
Encrypting text	0	0	0	0	1367	0	0	0	0	998
Decrypting text	594	1413	1160	1274	501	1084	1378	1508	502	0

In our analysis of encryption algorithms for managing pet health records, RSA, known for its asymmetric encryption, displayed significant variability in performance metrics. Particularly, the time required for key generation showed substantial fluctuations, with recorded times as short as 75,356 microseconds, and as long as 301,008 microseconds in some tests. Furthermore, the encryption and decryption processes for image data also revealed considerable time consumption, with decryption durations often exceeding 250,000 microseconds. These observations indicate that while RSA offers robust security features, its relatively slow operational speed poses potential challenges in terms of computational efficiency, which could impact the overall performance of our pet health record management system (Table 2).

In our study on encryption methods for securing pet health records, the RC4 algorithm showed very low encryption and decryption times for both image and text data, with several measurements nearly approaching zero microseconds. These results suggest that RC4 could enhance transaction processing speed within our system. However, the security strength of RC4 does not match that of more modern encryption algorithms, which raises concerns about its suitability. This discrepancy between RC4's high speed and lower security level might

Table 2. RC4 Performance for Image and text Data in Microseconds

RC4 (image)	1	2	3	4	5	6	7	8	9	10
Encrypting image	107	0	0	0	171	0	543	0	0	0
Decrypting image	0	0	664	0	0	0	0	0	1502	0
Encrypting text	0	0	0	0	0	0	0	0	0	0
Decrypting text	0	0	0	0	0	0	0	0	0	0

restrict its use in our pet health record management system, where maintaining data integrity and security is crucial (Table 3).

Table 3. DES Performance for Image and text Data in Microseconds

DES (image)	1	2	3	4	5	6	7	8	9	10
Encrypting image	1073	540	820	1047	1091	708	1217	599	1121	1024
Decrypting image	1058	551	0	819	606	999	1005	1018	501	0
Encrypting text	0	0	0	0	0	0	0	0	0	0
Decrypting text	0	0	0	0	0	508	0	0	0	0

In evaluating encryption algorithms for managing pet health records, we noted that DES displayed moderate processing times, with encryption of image data taking between 540 to 1,217 microseconds and decryption times ranging up to 1,058 microseconds. These figures suggest that DES could offer operational benefits due to its processing speed. However, the well-known security vulnerabilities associated with DES could deter its adoption in our system. The risk of compromised data integrity due to these vulnerabilities may outweigh the potential benefits of faster processing times in managing sensitive pet health records (Table 4).

Table 4. Chacha20 Performance for Image and text Data in Microseconds

CHACHA20 (image)	1	2	3	4	5	6	7	8	9	10
Encrypting image	501	0	0	109	0	0	0	0	0	101
Decrypting image	0	584	511	0	0	668	0	634	0	0
Encrypting text	0	0	0	0	0	0	0	0	0	0
Decrypting text	0	0	0	0	0	508	0	0	0	0

In our assessment of encryption methods suitable for managing pet health records, ChaCha20 demonstrated a promising balance of speed and security. For instance, it took only 501 microseconds to encrypt image data during our initial trial, with decryption times also proving to be efficient, albeit with some variability. Such performance indicates that ChaCha20 might be an effective option for securing metadata within pet health record systems, given its ability to quickly process data while maintaining a strong security posture. This could make it a practical choice for ensuring the integrity and confidentiality of sensitive health information in a veterinary setting (Table 5).

Table 5. Blowfish Performance for Image and text Data in Microseconds

blowfish (image)	1	2	3	4	5	6	7	8	9	10
Encrypting image	542	603	506	599	507	1145	608	1137	633	541
Decrypting image	0	0	508	512	501	501	1037	999	575	532
Encrypting text	0	0	537	520	0	533	91	0	0	0
Decrypting text	0	0	0	0	0	0	0	0	0	0

In our exploration of encryption algorithms for pet health record management, Blowfish exhibited moderate performance, with encryption times for image data ranging between 506 to 1,145 microseconds. Although Blowfish has been historically recognized for providing a reasonable balance of speed and security, the development of newer algorithms with improved security capabilities could diminish its appeal for modern systems. This raises questions about the adequacy of Blowfish in safeguarding sensitive pet health information against the evolving landscape of cybersecurity threats (Table 6).

Table 6. AES Performance for Image and text Data in Microseconds

AES (image)	1	2	3	4	5	6	7	8	9	10
Encrypting image	0	360	0	82	592	608	502	541	510	513
Decrypting image	1332	0	1005	0	504	0	0	0	0	0
Encrypting text	0	0	0	0	0	0	0	507	0	0
Decrypting text	0	0	0	0	0	0	0	0	0	0

In our evaluation of encryption algorithms for the management of pet health records, AES showed strong performance and reliability. This algorithm achieved encryption of image data in as little as zero microseconds in some instances, with decryption times also being impressively low, exemplified by a 504-microsecond decryption time in one of the trials. Recognized for its robust security features, AES's consistent performance in both speed and security makes it a compelling choice for enhancing the protection and efficiency of our pet health record system.

This ensures that sensitive health data remains secure while facilitating quick access when needed.

The data we've gathered provides valuable insights into the suitability of various encryption algorithms for managing pet health records within a blockchain-based system. We are evaluating six encryption methods-RSA, RC4, DES, ChaCha20, Blowfish, and AES-to find an optimal balance between security and operational efficiency. Our system, which relies on smart contracts and encrypted NFTs to manage and secure records, demands an encryption approach that aligns with the dynamic nature of veterinary care, characterized by frequent and diverse transactions. Our extensive testing and analysis aim to ensure that the chosen encryption method not only meets stringent security requirements but also supports the swift operational pace necessary for effective pet health record management. This approach is crucial for maintaining a reliable and transparent system that veterinarians and pet owners can trust.

5 Evaluation Scenarios

5.1 Analysis of Encrypted NFTs

The process for creating an encrypted Non-Fungible Token (NFT) and uploading it to the InterPlanetary File System (IPFS) involves a series of detailed steps, which are clearly outlined with both visual aids and code-based examples. The first step is to organize the essential pet health record data into a digital format. This organization is demonstrated in a code snippet that specifies the health data parameters such as the type of test, the results, and important timestamps, as shown in Fig. 2. The structure of this data is carefully designed to meet the criteria for an NFT, making sure that each component of the pet's health record is properly captured and represented.

The final step in managing pet health records involves the retrieval and decryption of the NFT data from IPFS, as shown through a browser interface that displays the decrypted health record (Fig. 3). This decrypted data is formatted to be human-readable, facilitating both verification and review by authorized individuals. This step confirms the system's ability to successfully decrypt and grant access to the pet health record, emphasizing the methodical and secure approach to record management. This sequence ensures that the entire process, from encryption and storage to retrieval, upholds the principles of security and reliability critical to managing sensitive health information.

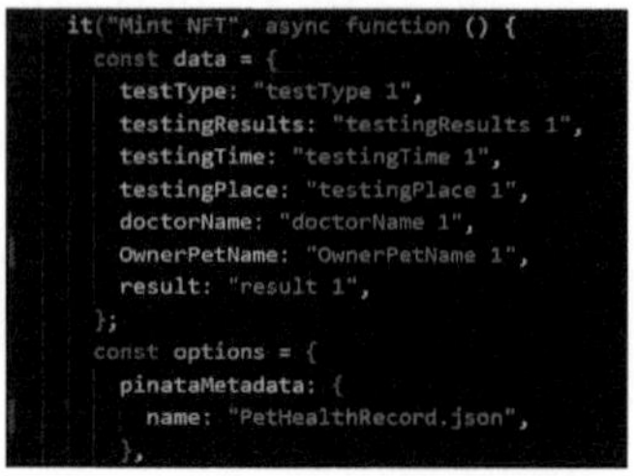

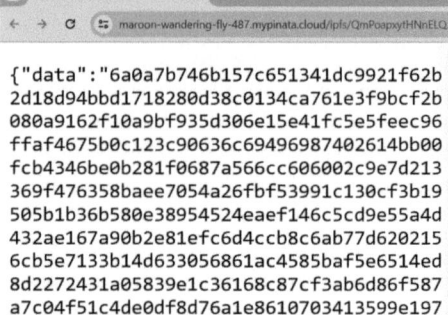

Fig. 2. Code Snippet Illustrating the Data Structure and Metadata for RSA-Encrypted NFT Creation.

Fig. 3. IPFS Representing the Encrypted NFT Metadata.

5.2 Testing on EVM-Supported Platforms

The Ethereum Virtual Machine (EVM) is vital for executing smart contracts across blockchain networks. In our project to secure pet health records, we used EVM-compatible platforms such as Binance Smart Chain, Polygon, Fantom, and Celo due to their ability to support key system functions. Our evaluation focused on three main areas: recording new pet health records on the blockchain, minting NFTs for each record, and transferring these NFTs within the network. We assessed the transaction speed, computational needs, user interface, and security of each platform to ensure they could handle the regular use by veterinary professionals and the safe transfer of sensitive health data among various stakeholders.

Table 7. Transaction fee

	Transaction Creation	Create NFT	Transfer NFT
BNB	0.0273134 BNB ($8.27)	0.00109162 BNB ($0.33)	0.00057003 BNB ($0.17)
Fantom	0.00957754 FTM ($0.00)	0.000405167 FTM ($0.00)	0.0002380105 FTM ($0.00)
Polygon	0.006840710032835408 MATIC ($0.01)	0.000289405001852192 MATIC ($0.00)	0.000170007501088048 MATIC ($0.00)
Celo	0.007097844 CELO ($0.005)	0.0002840812 CELO ($0.000)	0.0001554878 CELO ($0.000)

The Table 7 provides a comparative analysis of transaction fees on different blockchain platforms, essential for operating a system designed to secure pet health records through encrypted NFTs and smart contracts. The platforms evaluated include Binance Smart Chain (BNB), Fantom (FTM), Polygon (MATIC), and Celo (CELO), chosen for their compatibility with the Ethereum Virtual Machine (EVM). This compatibility is vital for implementing the smart contracts key to our system. The table also includes a summary of the token valuations for these platforms as of June 19, 2024, at 9:00:00 AM UTC, offering insight into the financial context in which these networks operate. Transaction fees are crucial as they cover the computational costs involved in processing and validating transactions, with specific implications for transaction creation, NFT creation, and NFT transfer within our pet health record management system.

On the Binance Smart Chain (BSC), creating a blockchain entry, which is necessary for recording new health events in pet records, costs 0.0273134 BNB, or about $8.27. This fee covers transactions like admitting a new pet to a clinic or updating a health record. Minting an NFT, used for creating a digital version of a pet's health record, costs 0.00109162 BNB, or $0.33. Transferring an NFT, which may be needed when ownership of the health record changes, costs 0.00057003 BNB, or roughly $0.17. These costs reflect BSC's pricing for managing these digital transactions.

The Fantom network offers a significantly lower fee structure, with costs for initiating a blockchain transaction, creating an NFT, and transferring an NFT at 0.00957754 FTM, 0.000405167 FTM, and 0.0002380105 FTM, respectively. These minimal fees translate into negligible dollar amounts, making Fantom an economical choice for managing pet health record transactions such as updating treatment details or transferring records between veterinary practices.

Polygon provides an economical solution with its transaction fees for logging entries, minting NFTs, and transferring NFTs at 0.006840710032835408 MATIC, 0.000289405001852192 MATIC, and 0.000170007501088048 MATIC, respectively. These low charges, amounting to just cents, make it an appropriate platform for conducting a high volume of transactions in the management of pet health records without incurring substantial costs. This affordability is crucial for frequent updates and interactions within the veterinary care system, ensuring that the flow of information and management of records remains cost-effective.

Celo also presents a competitive fee structure suitable for low-cost operations in pet health record management, with fees for creating entries at 0.007097844 CELO, and for minting and transferring NFTs at 0.0002840812 CELO and 0.0001554878 CELO, respectively. These minimal costs, all less than a cent, highlight Celo's capability to support the demands of frequent and varied transactions typical in managing pet health records. The platform's ability to facilitate numerous transactions at minimal expense makes it a viable option for ensuring efficient and transparent handling of pet health data.

This comparative analysis of transaction fees across different blockchain platforms is crucial for assessing the costs involved in managing pet health records using smart contracts and encrypted NFTs. Each platform-Binance Smart Chain, Fantom, Polygon, and Celo-offers a unique cost structure that could significantly impact the choice of blockchain, particularly in large-scale systems where frequent transactions are expected. Veterinary practices and pet health record management systems must carefully consider these fees to ensure the economic viability of their operations. Balancing these costs with the need for robust security, provided by encryption algorithms like RSA, RC4, DES, ChaCha20, Blowfish, and

6 Conclusion

Our investigation underscores the viability of using blockchain technology, combined with smart contracts, encrypted NFTs, and IPFS, to substantially improve the management of child health records. The deployment of various encryption algorithms ensures robust data security and maintains the integrity and privacy of the records. By testing this system across multiple blockchain platforms, we have validated its flexibility and operational efficiency. This study confirms that our proposed framework provides a secure, efficient, and cost-effective solution for managing sensitive health data, which could significantly benefit stakeholders within the healthcare sector. Moving forward, continued refinement and adoption of this technology could facilitate widespread improvements in health record management practices.

References

1. Aigner, et al.: Prototypical implementation of an animal health record (AHR) for livestock management. Ph.D. thesis (2014)
2. Anholt, et al.: Mining free-text medical records for companion animal enteric syndrome surveillance. Prev. Vet. Med. **113**(4), 417–422 (2014)
3. Anholt, et al.: Spatial-temporal clustering of companion animal enteric syndrome: detection and investigation through the use of electronic medical records from participating private practices. Epidemiol. Infect. **143**(12), 2547–2558 (2015)
4. Anholt, R.: Informatics and the electronic medical record for syndromic surveillance in companion animals: development, application and utility. Ph.D. thesis, University of Calgary (2013)
5. Bang, N., et al.: Blockchain-enhanced IoHT: a patient-centric internet of healthcare things platform with smart contract-driven data management. In: International Conference on Advances in Mobile Computing and Multimedia Intelligence, pp. 50–56. Springer (2023)
6. Duong-Trung, N., et al.: On components of a patient-centered healthcare system using smart contract. In: Proceedings of the 2020 4th International Conference on Cryptography, Security and Privacy, pp. 31–35 (2020)
7. Duong-Trung, N., et al.: Smart care: integrating blockchain technology into the design of patient-centered healthcare systems. In: Proceedings of the 2020 4th International Conference on Cryptography, Security and Privacy, pp. 105–109 (2020)
8. Gates, et al.: Assessing obesity in adult dogs and cats presenting for routine vaccination appointments in the north island of new Zealand using electronic medical records data. New Zealand Vet. J. **67**(3), 126–133 (2019)
9. Gray, et al.: Using electronic health records to explore negotiations around euthanasia decision making for dogs and cats in the UK. Vet. Record **190**(9) (2022)

10. Hanauer, D.A., Ramakrishnan, N., Seyfried, L.S.: Describing the relationship between cat bites and human depression using data from an electronic health record. PLoS ONE **8**(8), e70585 (2013)
11. Kass, et al.: Syndromic surveillance in companion animals utilizing electronic medical records data: development and proof of concept. PeerJ **4**, e1940 (2016)
12. Kim, et al.: Major medical causes by breed and life stage for dogs presented at veterinary clinics in the republic of Korea: a survey of electronic medical records. PeerJ **6**, e5161 (2018)
13. Krone, et al.: Survey of electronic veterinary medical record adoption and use by independent small animal veterinary medical practices in massachusetts. J. Am. Vet. Med. Assoc. **245**(3), 324–332 (2014)
14. Le, H.T., et al.: Patient-chain: patient-centered healthcare system a blockchain-based technology in dealing with emergencies. In: International Conference on Parallel and Distributed Computing: Applications and Technologies, pp. 576–583. Springer (2021)
15. Menéndez, et al.: Data quality of animal health records on swiss dairy farms. Vet. Rec. **163**(8), 241–246 (2008)
16. Nam, T., et al.: SPaMeR: securing patient medical records in the cloud-a microservice and Brokerless architecture approach. In: International Conference on Web Services, pp. 32–46. Springer (2023)
17. Quintana, et al.: Exploratory analysis of animal bites events in the city of Buenos Aires using data from electronic health records. In: Digital Personalized Health and Medicine, pp. 1283–1284. IOS Press (2020)
18. Romar, et al.: Fine-grained access control in an animal health record. Ph.D. thesis, Wien (2018)
19. Salt, et al.: Stratification of companion animal life stages from electronic medical record diagnosis data. J. Gerontol. Ser. A **78**(4), 579–586 (2023)

Resource Allocation in Multi-Fog/Cloud Systems Using a Hybrid Genetic Algorithm-Reinforcement Learning Approach

Masoud Mokhtari and Sudhakar Ganti[✉]

Computer Science Department, University of Victoria, Victoria, Canada
{masoudmokhtari,sganti}@uvic.ca

Abstract. This research paper presents a new method for tackling resource allocation challenges in multi-Fog and Cloud systems with varying demands, leveraging reinforcement learning. Our approach is structured in two phases: first, we identify the optimal Fog node for resource allocation, and in the second phase, reinforcement learning is applied to determine the best long-term strategy for whether the selected Fog node should handle tasks locally or offload them to the Cloud. To improve convergence speed, we integrate a Genetic Algorithm (GA) into the reinforcement learning process. The goal is to maximize Fog resource utilization while considering the number of resource blocks and each request's maximum delay tolerance. Experimental evaluations confirm the effectiveness of our method in enhancing resource allocation within Fog computing environments. We benchmark our approach against pure Reinforcement Learning (RL) approach in dynamic resource allocation scenarios, with results showing that the combined approach outperforms others in speed, resource utilization, and load balancing.

Keywords: Reinforcement Learning · Resource Allocation · Fog Computing · Cloud Computing

1 Introduction

The Internet of Things (IoT) enables seamless data exchange among devices, fostering smart services and informed decision-making [1,2]. While Cloud computing has traditionally supported IoT data storage and processing, the increase in data traffic has resulted in network congestion, highlighting its limitations. Fog computing addresses this issue by bringing processing, storage, and control closer to IoT devices, enhancing quality of service (QoS) and alleviating Cloud-based challenges [3].

As an intermediary layer, Fog computing supplements Cloud resources by offering localized services, yet Fog nodes themselves face resource constraints. Effective resource allocation is critical, requiring decisions on whether tasks should be processed locally at the Fog node or offloaded to the Cloud, depending on the QoS requirements of each application [4].

Our contribution focuses on dynamically allocating Fog resources across nodes to meet user demands, thereby achieving load balancing and adaptability. While Cloud computing provides essential infrastructure, Fog computing is vital for supporting latency-sensitive IoT applications by reducing delays and easing data congestion.

This document is structured as follows: Sect. 2 reviews relevant literature in this field. Section 3 outlines the resource allocation problem and the Fog node selection process. Section 4 provides an overview of the system architecture. In Sect. 5, we introduce our proposed Reinforcement Learning solution to the resource allocation issue described in Sect. 3. Our analysis and experimental results are presented in Sect. 6. Finally, Sect. 7 concludes with recommendations for future research.

2 Literature Review

The literature on Fog computing emphasizes the importance of latency-sensitive applications and quality-of-service (QoS) optimization. A typical Fog architecture includes three layers-Edge, Fog, and Cloud-that facilitate real-time interactions, low latency, and mobility, supporting applications such as e-health, vehicular communication, and industrial monitoring [5,6].

Task scheduling is critical to optimizing performance and resource efficiency. Karimi et al. [7] proposed using deep reinforcement learning for task scheduling between Multi-access Edge Computing (MEC) and the Cloud to achieve optimal task placement. Similarly, Bukhari et al. [8] focused on reducing latency, energy consumption, and response times. Dynamic scheduling and resource allocation techniques, especially at the Fog layer, help maintain QoS under network disruptions [8,9].

Various methods address scheduling challenges, including fuzzy logic for managing environmental unpredictability in Fog systems, as demonstrated by Parimi et al. [10], who achieved shorter wait times. Fonseca et al. [11] applied Integer Linear Programming (ILP) to minimize execution time and makespan, while other ILP approaches [12] also aim to enhance application performance by reducing processing time and costs.

Energy efficiency is a priority in Fog systems, especially those with battery-powered devices. Hosseinioun et al. [15] introduced a hybrid algorithm utilizing Dynamic Voltage and Frequency Scaling (DVFS) for energy-aware task scheduling, addressing bandwidth usage, latency, and energy consumption [16].

Reinforcement learning (RL) has shown promise in scheduling optimization within Fog environments. Farhat et al. [18] used RL to adapt to user demands and spatial-temporal variables, while Shi et al. [19] employed Deep Reinforcement Learning (DRL) in Vehicle-to-Vehicle communication, enhancing scheduling and reducing delays in vehicular networks.

In summary, optimizing task scheduling in Fog computing presents intricate challenges that necessitate innovative approaches. Techniques such as reinforcement learning, fuzzy logic, and hybrid algorithms hold promise for efficient resource utilization and fulfilling diverse application requirements. However, further research is needed to address emerging issues such as energy efficiency, dynamic resource allocation, network resilience, and comprehensive system-level strategies for effective scheduling.

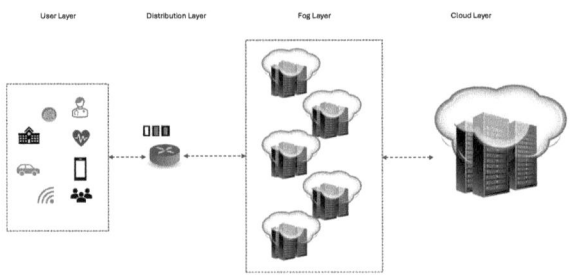

Fig. 1. System.

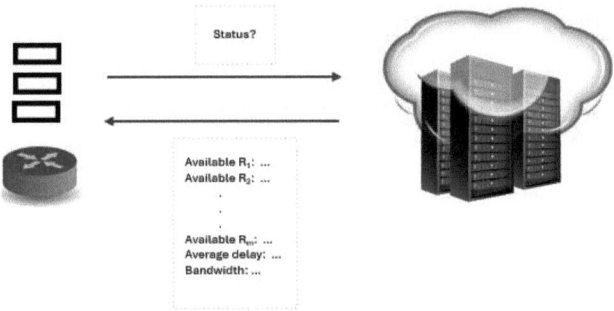

Fig. 2. Status Update.

3 Problem Statement

The rise of Fog computing has revolutionized resource management by emphasizing the proximity of computational resources to the network edge. In dynamic environments, efficient resource allocation is essential to meeting user demands while addressing challenges like limited resources and the need for low-latency applications. Users express their requirements in a tuple-based format, specifying the desired resources, maximum allowable delay, and service duration.

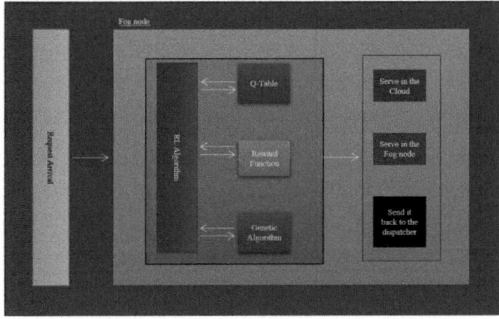

Fig. 3. Resource Allocation in the Fog node.

This paper presents a framework for task scheduling that employs reinforcement learning to tackle task allocation and scheduling challenges within Fog and Cloud environments. The scenario is structured as follows: there are n Fog nodes, labeled $F_1, F_2, \ldots, F_n$, each containing multiple resources represented as $(R_1, R_2, \ldots, R_m)$, where m indicates the types of resources available, each with a defined maximum capacity.

User requests are submitted in tuple format, $(u_1, u_2, \ldots, u_k, d_{\max}, L)$, where u_1 to u_k represent the resource needs, $d_{\max}$ is the maximum acceptable delay, and L is the service duration. Each request is unique and indivisible, requiring the system to decide whether to process it within the Fog or offload it to the Cloud. If processed in the Fog, an appropriate Fog node is selected.

Resource allocation takes place in a complex state space influenced by the diverse types of resources. Evaluating resource availability and latency at each Fog node is crucial to meet delay constraints and to make decisions on Fog versus Cloud processing. Efficiently distributing tasks among Fog nodes requires a load-balancing approach to prevent node overload, reduce delay, and align with user expectations.

Achieving these objectives involves strategic trade-offs. While processing tasks within the Fog network is preferred, preventing node overload is necessary to maintain resource efficiency and system reliability. Requests should be distributed across nodes to minimize bottlenecks, especially when only a few nodes are available.

The goal is to optimize the performance of the Fog network and minimize reliance on the Cloud. When Fog resources are limited, tasks can be redirected to the Cloud to sustain efficiency. By balancing resources, reducing delays, and preserving stability, the network effectively meets user requirements within its constraints.

4 System Architecture

Figure 1 illustrates the system architecture designed to manage user requests efficiently. In this setup, users submit requests, which are received by a distributor node acting as an intermediary. This distributor queues incoming requests for processing and maintains a status table of Fog node resource availability and workload (Fig. 2). The status table enables the distributor to allocate requests based on each node's current capacity, ensuring efficient resource utilization across the Fog network.

4.1 Request Processing in Fog and Cloud

Requests may be processed by either a Fog node or the Cloud, depending on the following conditions:

1. **Unsatisfiable Requests at the Fog Level**: If none of the Fog nodes can meet the resource demands of a request-due to resource constraints or high workload-the distributor routes it to the Cloud. This decision is informed by periodic Fog node status updates, which provide real-time resource availability. Directing such requests to the Cloud ensures timely processing when Fog nodes are insufficiently resourced, thus preventing service degradation.
2. **Reward-Based Offloading to the Cloud**: A Fog node may also decide to offload a request to the Cloud based on its reward function, which considers processing cost, potential penalties, and system performance. If local processing is inefficient or risks overloading the system, offloading to the Cloud helps maintain optimal performance.

In both scenarios, offloading to the Cloud is a strategic choice aimed at balancing resource efficiency and service quality. The Cloud is assumed to have adequate resources to fulfill any forwarded request, making transmission delay the primary factor for Cloud routing decisions. This consideration aligns with user-defined delay requirements to maintain QoS.

4.2 Enhancing Distribution in Fog Computing

Efficient request distribution in Fog Computing goes beyond mere resource availability. While the distributor currently focuses on minimizing propagation delay, it also considers factors like distance, bandwidth, and network conditions. Once a Fog node is selected, the request is evaluated against the node's available resources, including CPU, memory, and storage. Each Fog node updates the distributor with metrics such as average delay and recent request sizes, providing deeper insights into its performance and resource usage patterns.

In the next phase of task scheduling, the distributor retrieves tasks for processing by the selected Fog nodes. At this stage, a reinforcement learning (RL) algorithm (illustrated in Fig. 3) helps each Fog node determine whether to process a request locally or in the Cloud. Each Fog node hosts multiple resource types, $R_1, R_2, \ldots, R_m$, and makes allocation decisions based on real-time resource availability.

4.3 Request Allocation Process

The time required to allocate a request includes the following components:

1. **Waiting Time in the Distributor Queue**: Requests wait in the queue based on factors like system load and priority. Queue length can affect waiting times.
2. **Propagation Delay**: After the distributor selects a request, it sends it to a Fog node, incurring a propagation delay that depends on the distance and network speed.

4.4 Resource Allocation Algorithm

Algorithm 1 describes the allocation process. It initializes the distributor queue Q and creates a list of Fog nodes that can potentially serve each request. For each request, the algorithm evaluates the resource demands and compares them against available resources in each node. If a node cannot meet a request, another node is evaluated until a match is found.

If no suitable Fog node is available, the algorithm calculates the Cloud delay; if this delay is within the user's maximum delay tolerance, the request is sent to the Cloud. Otherwise, it remains in the queue. When a suitable Fog node is available, the request is forwarded to the node based on its potential (Selection-1) calculated in Eq. (1) or the minimum delay (Selection-2) calculated in Eq. (2).

$$\text{potential}_i = \left(\frac{\prod R'_{i,k}}{P_i \times \text{AvgDelay}_i} \right) \qquad (1)$$

where $R'_{i,k} \neq 0$ is the remaining amount of resource k in Fog node i, and P_i represents the number of times the node has been selected.

$$D_{i,j} = (\text{Waiting Time in Queue} + \text{Propagation Delay}_{i,j}) \qquad (2)$$

where $D_{i,j}$ represents the delay experienced by request i if served by Fog node j. Equation (1) distributes the workload effectively, balancing the number of selections across nodes to avoid overload, thereby optimizing resource usage and meeting service demands.

5 RL Approach

The state space S of the Fog node comprises a finite set representing potential allocations of various resource types. If we denote the different resource types as $R_1, R_2, \ldots, R_m$, where m is the total number of resource types, then the state space consists of $|R_1 + 1| \times |R_2 + 1| \times \ldots \times |R_m + 1|$ states. In other words, each resource type can range from being fully unoccupied to being fully occupied.

The action space A consists of two potential actions: remaining within the Fog node for local processing or transmitting data to the Cloud for processing.

Guided by the best policy it has learned, the algorithm determines the most suitable action among these options.

In the process of Q-learning, immediate feedback in the form of rewards or penalties plays a crucial role. These signals provide the scheduler with valuable information regarding the quality of its actions. By analyzing these rewards or penalties, the scheduler adjusts its decision-making strategy, progressively enhancing its performance through successive interactions with the environment.

For example, when a specific action results in a positive reward, the scheduler learns that the action was advantageous and becomes more inclined to repeat it under similar circumstances in the future. Conversely, if an action yields a negative reward, the scheduler learns to avoid it in comparable situations. Over time, through this continuous feedback loop, the scheduler refines its decision-making process, ultimately converging towards an optimal policy for task scheduling.

Algorithm 1 : Fog node Selection Algorithm

1: **Initialize:** Number of Fog nodes n, $Q = \emptyset$, $FognodeList = \emptyset$, Resource type m, Resource vector u
2: **while** $|Q| \neq 0$ **do**
3:   Retrieve the first request j, gather all attributes, and place them in u
4:   **for** $i = 1$ to n **do**
5:     $canAllocate \leftarrow true$
6:     **for** $k = 1$ to m **do**
7:       **if** $(R_k < u_k)$ **then**
8:         $canAllocate \leftarrow false$
9:         break
10:      **end if**
11:    **end for**
12:    **if** $canAllocate$ **then**
13:      Compute estimated delay $D_{i,j}$ with (2)
14:      Add Fog node i to $FognodeList$ with computed delay $D_{i,j}$
15:    **end if**
16: **end for**
17: **if** $FognodeList = \emptyset$ **then**
18:    Compute delay to the Cloud $D_{Cloud,j}$ with (2)
19:    **if** $D_{Cloud,j} > u[m+1]$ **then**
20:      Send request j back to Q
21:    **else**
22:      Send request j to the Cloud and remove it from Q
23:    **end if**
24: **else**
25:    **Selection-1:**
26:      Assign request j to Fog node i with the biggest value calculated by (1)
27:    **Selection-2:**
28:      Assign request j to Fog node i with the smallest value calculated by (2)
29:    Remove request j from Q
30: **end if**
31: **end while**

Algorithm (1) referred to as the Selection Algorithm, is designed to efficiently allocate incoming requests to available Fog nodes while considering resource constraints and estimated delays. Initially, it initializes several parameters, including the number of Fog nodes n, a request queue Q, and a resource vector u that captures the attributes of the incoming request. The algorithm processes requests in a loop, where it retrieves the first request and checks each Fog node to determine whether it can allocate the necessary resources. For each Fog node, if the available resources are insufficient to meet the request's requirements, it marks that node as unable to allocate. If a Fog node can satisfy the request, the algorithm calculates the estimated delay for that node and adds it to a list of eligible Fog nodes.

If no Fog nodes can accommodate the request, the algorithm calculates the delay to the Cloud. If the Cloud's delay exceeds the request's tolerance, it returns the request to the queue for further consideration. Conversely, if the delay is acceptable, it routes the request to the Cloud. When multiple Fog nodes are available, the algorithm employs one of two selection strategies: either assigning the request to the Fog node with the highest value based on a selection criterion or to the node with the smallest estimated delay. This approach ensures that requests are handled efficiently, balancing resource allocation in fog computing with the option of Cloud processing when necessary.

$$r_k = \zeta \sqrt{\prod_{i=1}^{m} \frac{N_i - S_{(i)}}{req_i}} + \theta \sqrt{\frac{d_{prop}}{delay_i}} \qquad (3)$$

To assess the quality of requests, we implement a reward system that considers two main factors: resource utilization and propagation delay (3). Once Algorithm (1) selects a Fog node, Algorithm (2) calculates the reward for each request k (r_k) by taking a weighted sum of these factors. The weights (ζ and θ), which total 1, represent the importance of each factor and can be adjusted to suit the requirements of different scenarios. This flexible approach allows for a tailored, context-aware evaluation of request quality.

1. **Resource Utilization Factor**: This measures efficiency by comparing the remaining resources of each type to the requested quantity. Specifically, it considers the maximum resource N_i, the occupied resources $S_{(i)}$, and the requested amount req_i. A higher ratio indicates better resource utilization, positively impacting the reward.
2. **Propagation Delay Factor**: This assesses the delay caused by the request, focusing on the ratio of propagation delay d_{prop} to the requested amount $delay_i$. A lower ratio is preferable.

Combining these factors with appropriate weights, our reward system encourages optimizing resource utilization while minimizing propagation delay. Adjusting the weights helps prioritize different aspects in the scheduling process.

Algorithm (2) combines Q-learning with a genetic algorithm (GA) to optimize decision-making in a system with delay-sensitive tasks, like fog/Cloud computing. It initializes parameters for exploration (ε), discount factor (γ), and Q-values for each state-action pair. In each episode, it chooses actions based on an

Algorithm 2 : Hybrid (RL/GA) Algorithm

1: **Initialize** $\{\gamma, \varepsilon\} \in [0, 1]$
2: **Input** $N, Episodes, Q$
3: **Initialize** $N = (N_1, N_2, N_3, ..., N_u)$
4: **Initialize** states: $Q(s, a) \ \forall (s, a) \in Q$
5: **Initialize** $d_{avg}, j = 0$
6: **for** $i = 0$ to $Episodes - 1$ **do**
7:     $e \leftarrow$ Generate a random number from $(0, 1]$
8:     $req \leftarrow$ Read a user's Request
9:     $delay_i \leftarrow$ Read a user's Delay Tolerance
10:     Given the current State S
11:     **if** $e \leq \varepsilon$ **then**
12:       **Q-Learning:**
13:       Take a random action a_t, calculate r_t based on (3)
14:       and store s_{t+1}
15:       **Genetic Algorithm:**
16:       Take a action a_t based on (1),
17:       calculate r_t based on (3) and store s_{t+1}
18:       d = Calculate $D_{Fog,i}$ based on (2)
19:     **else if** (for all $req_i \in req : N_i - S_{(i)} - req_i \geq 0$) and ($D_{\text{Fog},i} \leq delay_i$) **then**
20:       Serve in Fog: Take the action a_t and calculate r_t based on (3) and store s_{t+1}
21:     **else**
22:       d = Calculate $D_{Cloud,i}$ based on (2)
23:       **if** $D_{\text{Cloud},i} \leq delay_i$ **then**
24:         serve in Cloud:
25:         Calculate r_t based on (3) and $s_{t+1} = s_t$
26:         continue
27:       **end if**
28:       $q_{t+1} \leftarrow 0$
29:       **for** each a_{t+1} in actions **do**
30:         $q_{t+1} \leftarrow q_{t+1} + (P(a_{t+1}|s_{t+1}) \cdot Q(s_{t+1}, a_{t+1}))$
31:       **end for**
32:       $G \leftarrow r_t + \gamma \cdot \max Q(s_{t+1}, a_{t+1})$
33:       $Q(s_t, a_t) \leftarrow Q(s_t, a_t) + \alpha \cdot G$
34:       Update Q with $Q(s_t, a_t)$
35:       **if** $Q(s_t, a_t)$ converges for all (s, a) **then**
36:         break
37:       **end if**
38:     **end if**
39: **end for**

ε-greedy strategy: if a randomly generated value is within ε, it explores by taking a random action (Q-learning) or applies a GA for action selection. Otherwise, it checks if requests can be served in the fog (if delay tolerance and resource availability are sufficient); if not, it evaluates Cloud processing feasibility.

The algorithm updates Q-values based on observed rewards and the estimated value of future actions, refining the Q-table to improve decision quality over time. It breaks out of the loop once Q-values converge, ensuring the learned policy is stable. This approach effectively balances exploration and exploitation, making it well-suited for dynamic, delay-sensitive environments.

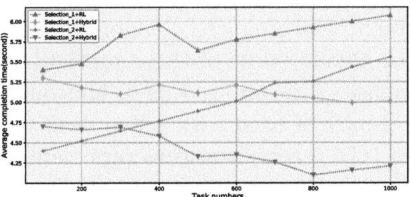

Fig. 4. Average task completion time.

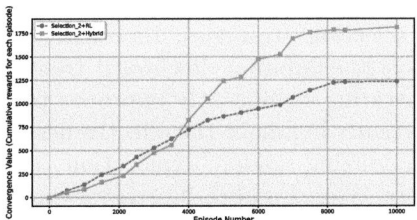

Fig. 5. Average Number of Tasks served by the Cloud.

6 Analysis and Results

To assess the efficacy of the proposed algorithm, we simulated task scheduling within a multi-Fog/Cloud computing environment. Our simulation encompassed scenarios with 100 to 1000 requests in increments of 100, each with randomly generated lengths between 500 and 3000. The environment featured ten Fog nodes and a Cloud node, with each Fog node offering five distinct types of resources. To ensure precision, we averaged the results from multiple trials, with the average based on twenty repetitions. Notably, we found that increasing the number of trials beyond fifteen had negligible impact on the average outcomes. Additionally, We ensured fair comparisons by maintaining constants for ζ and θ at 0.5.

In our experimental methodology, which consisted of two phases. The first phase involved employing priority task scheduling methods (Selection-1 and Selection-2) and benchmarking them against RR and Random task scheduling during the initial task allocation phase. The Random strategy allocates requests randomly between Fog nodes and the Cloud, serving as a baseline for comparison. The RR strategy follows a cyclic order, distributing tasks evenly among available nodes to prevent bottlenecks. Selection-1 allocates tasks using a specific formula defined in (2), optimizing resource allocation according to this algorithm's criteria. Selection-2 further refines this approach by choosing the node with the least delay among those selected by 1, aiming to minimize latency. In the next phase, we applied a reinforcement learning (RL) algorithm and a genetic algorithm (GA) to demonstrate the effectiveness of these methods across all the strategies analyzed in the initial phase. This allowed us to thoroughly evaluate the performance, efficiency, and latency of each task scheduling technique. In the context of the genetic algorithm (GA), requests were represented as chromosomes, and the fitness function was defined according to (1). For the selection process in generating the next population, we prioritized individuals with superior fitness function values. Additionally, we employed a uniform crossover mechanism and applied single-point mutation to introduce genetic diversity in the offspring.

Figure 4 critically analyzes the impact of increasing task volume on the average completion time of the entire system. As task numbers rise, the average completion time for the RL approach also increases, although the rate of increase varies across different selection strategies. In contrast, the hybrid algorithm, particularly for Selection-2, exhibits a downward trend, with both Selection-1 and Selection-2 demonstrating significantly improved performance over the RL-based methods. These results highlight the effectiveness of the advanced hybrid approach, which, by minimizing random exploration, achieves greater efficiency than the RL-based alternatives. Figure 5 illustrates the effect of increasing task numbers on the average number of tasks offloaded to the Cloud for processing. This figure compares the number of requests that different algorithms decide to offload to the Cloud. As observed, the hybrid algorithm-applied in both Selection-1 and Selection-2-outperforms the reinforcement learning (RL) approach. This improved performance is due to the hybrid algorithm's use of a genetic algorithm during the exploration phase, rather than relying on random decisions. By leveraging the genetic algorithm, the hybrid method achieves a more efficient exploration process, leading to more informed decision-making and overall superior outcomes. Figure 6 examines the impact of increasing task volume on load distribution across Fog nodes, with a particular focus on load balancing. Load balancing is assessed by comparing each node's resource usage to the average usage across all nodes. The load on each node is determined by the ratio of allocated to maximum available resources for each resource type, resulting in a normalized value between 0 and 1.

The average of these normalized values across all nodes, along with the standard deviation, provides a measure of resource usage balance. As illustrated in Fig. 6, while RL-based algorithms achieve reasonable load balancing, hybrid algorithms-specifically in both Selection-1 and Selection-2-demonstrate consistently superior load distribution. Additionally, it is worth noting that, within the number of generations and episodes used in our experiment, the standard

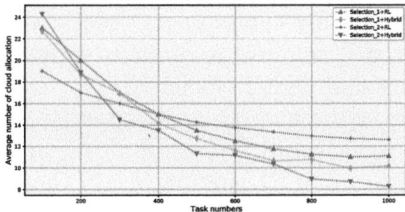

Fig. 6. Standard deviation of Fog nodes.

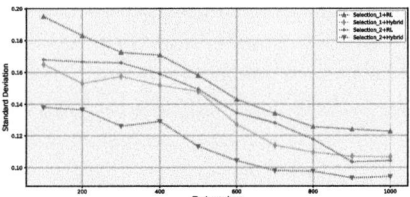

Fig. 7. Convergence.

deviation (SD) diagrams for the hybrid approach show a slight downward trend, indicating increasingly balanced resource usage.

Figure 7 presents a comparative analysis of the convergence behavior of the algorithms. To gain insights into the convergence process, we calculated the reward for each episode. Rather than plotting every data point, we selected key turning points to construct a more concise and insightful convergence curve. Minor fluctuations between these selected points were observed but are not emphasized here for clarity.

Our analysis of the convergence patterns indicates that the hybrid algorithm initially exhibited lower cumulative reward G than the RL-based approach. This aligns with expectations, as genetic algorithms (GAs) typically require more iterations to optimize effectively. However, as the convergence progresses, the rate of increase in cumulative reward for the hybrid algorithm surpasses that of the RL approach. It is important to note that this comparison focuses solely on Selection-2.

An interesting observation is that, while the cumulative reward for the hybrid algorithm ultimately exceeds that of the RL approach, there is a potential risk of convergence to local optima due to the nature of GAs. Finally, it is worth mentioning that these results represent averages across multiple iterations.

7 Conclusion

In conclusion, the proposed hybrid task scheduling algorithm for Fog/Cloud computing significantly improves performance compared to RL-based methods. It excels in load balancing, resource utilization, reduction of Cloud tasks, and average task completion time. By combining a genetic algorithm (GA) for exploration, the hybrid approach minimizes random exploration, leading to more informed decision-making and higher efficiency.

The hybrid algorithm shows a notable advantage in handling increasing task volumes. It consistently reduces task completion time and improves task offloading to the Cloud, outperforming RL approaches in these aspects. Furthermore, the hybrid method achieves superior load balancing, with more balanced resource usage across Fog nodes over time.

Though the hybrid algorithm initially has a slower convergence rate, it eventually surpasses the RL approach in cumulative reward, demonstrating its capacity for better long-term optimization. While there is a potential risk of convergence to local optima, the hybrid method's overall performance is significantly better, offering a scalable and efficient solution for task scheduling in Fog/Cloud environments.

References

1. Saleem, Y., Crespi, N., Rehmani, M.H., Copeland, R.: Internet of things-aided smart grid: technologies, architectures, applications, prototypes, and future research directions. IEEE Access **7**, 62962–63003 (2019)
2. Tran-Dang, H., Kim, D.: An information framework for Internet of Things services in physical internet. IEEE Access **6**, 43967–43977 (2018)
3. Mahmud, M.R., Srirama, S.N., Ramamohanarao, K., Buyya, R.: Profit-aware application placement for integrated fog-cloud computing environments. J. Parallel Distrib. Comput. **135**, 177–190 (2020)
4. Sarkar, S., Chatterjee, S., Misra, S.: Assessment of the suitability of fog computing in the context of Internet of Things. IEEE Trans. Cloud Comput. **6**(1), 46–59 (2018)
5. Nikolopoulos, V., Nikolaidou, M., Voreakou, M., Anagnostopoulos, D.: Fog node self-control middleware: enhancing context awareness towards autonomous decision making in fog colonies. Internet Things **19**, 100549 (2022)
6. Das, R., Inuwa, M.M.: A review on fog computing: issues, characteristics, challenges, and potential applications. Telemat. Inform. Rep. **10**, 100049 (2023)
7. Karimi, E., Chen, Y., Akbari, B.: Task offloading in vehicular edge computing networks via deep reinforcement learning. Comput. Commun. **189**, 193–204 (2022)
8. Bukhari, M., et al.: An intelligent proposed model for task offloading in fog-cloud collaboration using logistics regression. Comput. Intell. Neurosci. **2022**, 1–25 (2022)
9. Wang, J., et al.: Fast adaptive task offloading in edge computing based on meta reinforcement learning. IEEE Trans. Parallel Distrib. Syst. **32**, 242–253 (2021)
10. Ali, H., et al.: Real-time task scheduling in fog-cloud computing framework for IoT applications: a fuzzy logic based approach. In: Proceedings of 2021 International Conference on COMmunication Systems & NETworkS (COMSNETS), Bangalore, India, pp. 556–564 (2021)
11. Guevara, J., Fonseca, N.: Task scheduling in cloud-fog computing systems. Peer-Netw. Appl. **14**, 962–977 (2021)
12. Aburukba, R.O., et al.: Scheduling internet of things requests to minimize latency in hybrid fog-cloud computing. Future Gener. Comput. Syst. **111**, 539–551 (2020)

13. Abdulredha, M.N., Attea, B.A., Jabir, A.J.: An evolutionary algorithm for task scheduling problem in the cloud-fog environment. J. Phys: Conf. Ser. **1963**, 012044 (2021)
14. Tsai, J.F., Huang, C.H., Lin, M.H.: An optimal task assignment strategy in cloud-fog computing environment. Appl. Sci. **11**, 1909 (2021)
15. Hosseinioun, P., et al.: A new energy-aware tasks scheduling approach in fog computing using hybrid meta-heuristic algorithm. J. Parallel Distrib. Comput. **143**, 88–96 (2020)
16. Nikoui, T.S., et al.: Cost-aware task scheduling in fog-cloud environment. In: Proceedings of 2020 CSI/CPSSI International Symposium on Real-Time and Embedded Systems and Technologies (RTEST), Tehran, Iran, pp. 1–8 (2020)
17. Poltronieri, F., et al.: Reinforcement learning for value-based placement of fog services. In: Proceedings of 2021 IFIP/IEEE International Symposium on Integrated Network Management (IM), Bordeaux, France, pp. 466–472 (2021)
18. Farhat, P., Sami, H., Mourad, A.: Reinforcement r-learning model for time scheduling of on-demand fog placement. J. Supercomput. **76**, 1–23 (2020)
19. Shi, J., et al.: Deep reinforcement learning-based V2V partial computation offloading in vehicular fog computing. In: Proceedings of 2021 IEEE Wireless Communications and Networking Conference (WCNC), Nanjing, China, pp. 1–6 (2021)
20. Sutton, R.S., Barto, A.G.: Reinforcement Learning: An Introduction. MIT Press, MA, USA (1998)
21. Goudarzi, M., Palaniswami, M., Buyya, R.: A distributed deep reinforcement learning technique for application placement in edge and fog computing environments. IEEE Trans. Mob. Comput. **22**, 2491–2505 (2021)

Author Index

A
Aziz, Jamaluddin 32

B
Bang, L. K. 48, 62, 77

D
Deguara, Cedric 1

F
Farrugia, Franco 1

G
Ganti, Sudhakar 90
Gao, Jingbo 32
Gong, Yunbo 16

L
Li, Zhao 16
Liang, Qi 32

M
Mokhtari, Masoud 90

N
Ngan, K. T. N. 48, 62, 77

S
Sannusi, Shahrul Nazmi 32

T
Trong, N. Đ. P. 48, 62, 77
Trung, P. H. T. 48, 62, 77

Y
Yang, Ang 16

Author Index

MIX
Papier aus verantwortungsvollen Quellen
Paper from responsible sources
FSC® C105338

If you have any concerns about our products,
you can contact us on
ProductSafety@springernature.com

In case Publisher is established outside the EU,
the EU authorized representative is:
**Springer Nature Customer Service Center GmbH
Europaplatz 3, 69115 Heidelberg, Germany**

Printed by Libri Plureos GmbH
in Hamburg, Germany